Effective Presentation Skills

by

Robert B. Dilts

Meta Publications
P.O. Box 1910
Capitola, California 95010
(408) 464 - 0254
FAX (408) 464 - 0517

Library of Congress Card Number 94-76760
I.S.B.N. 0-916990-31-1

Contents

Part Two: Strategies Designing and Implementing Effective Presentations.

Part Three: Managing the Interpersonal Aspects of a Presentation.

Dedication

This book is dedicated to John Grinder
and Richard Bandler from whom I first
learned the art and joy of presenting; and
to Todd Epstein who has helped me to
turn that art into a science.

Acknowledgements

I would like to gratefully acknowledge my colleague and collaborator Gino Bonissone who contributed greatly to the underlying instructional methodology described in this book, and who spearheaded the project from which the material for this book was drawn.

I would also like to acknowledge Ivanna Gasperini for her invaluable theoretical and practical contributions and support.

I would like to thank Paulo DeNucci and the many people at the Italian National Railways who have taken the mission to be a 'learning organization' so seriously.

Many thanks also go to Michael Pollard who has worked with me so diligently on this and other projects in order to help me manifest my visions.

Preface

The material for this book is derived from one of a system of seminars which were designed for the Italian National Railways as part of its efforts to becoming a 'learning organization'. The system of seminars is made up of a path of four courses which form a complete trainer's training program:

1. Communication and Relational Skills for Presenters
2. Communication and Relational Skills for Instructors
3. Communication and Relational Skills for Trainers
4. Assessment Skills and Strategies for Trainers

The material for this book is taken from the support material for the first of these courses which focused on the communication and relational skills required to be an effective presenter. Readers familiar with my book *Skills For The Future* will notice some overlaps between certain concepts and processes written about in that work and the material in this book. Rather than be redundant, however, I think the similarities will help to enrich the reader's understanding and ability to apply the models and skills more easily.

This book is made up of twelve chapters emphasizing various key aspects of managing communication and relationships within the presentation context. The book has been organized into three parts which each emphasize a different basic dimension of designing, evaluating and implementing effective presentations.

The structure of the book has been designed to support as much as possible the assumptions, principles and methods of learning and presenting upon which it has been based. Each chapter begins with a brief overview of the chapter including its general objectives and the titles of the sections from which it is built. Each section contains 1) the basic conceptual material and/or learning activity for that section and 2) a summary of the section in the form of a 'storyboard' and the key points. A 'storyboard' is the essential ideas or concepts of the section arranged as they would be on an overhead transparency used during a course or presentation. 'Key points' are an attempt to capture the essential ideas and concepts expressed in each section. They summarize and encapsulate the micro level learning objectives for each section in as simple and direct a form as possible.

This structure allows the reader the choice to get the essence of section in a brief form if it is of less relevance or if he or she already has familiarity with the concepts, and wants to move on more quickly. Simply skimming the 'storyboards' and key points can provide you with a quick but comprehensive overview of each section.

Overview of the Book

The focus of this book is on communication and relational skills for presenters who operate in learning contexts. The basic purpose of the work is to 1) provide a cognitive structure and rationale for how to design communication strategies for effective presentations and 2) to provide some skills and strategies for managing the interactive and relational aspects of the presentation context. These skills and strategies revolve around the abilities to:

• Define clear goals and objectives
• Manage different learning styles
• Deal with different motivations and resistances

The main emphasis of the book will be on the application of these skills and strategies to facilitate the essential activities of a presenter in the learning context. Specifically,

• Designing presentations
• Selecting or creating the appropriate material
• Making effective presentations
• Handling questions from the audience
• Managing discussion in a group

The effective achievement of these activities requires the ability to understand and manage the relationship between a) communication, b) thinking styles, c) learning processes and d) group dynamics.

General Structure of the Book

The general framework for this book is to begin in Part 1 by covering some of the basic principles, frameworks and primary models for forming a communication strategy. Part 2 focuses on implementing those principles and models with respect to design of the topics, lessons and managing the conceptualizing and planning phase of a presentation. Part 3 focuses on the issues of motivation, relationship, resistance and the highly interpersonal aspects of presenting.

Goals of the Book

The basic goals of this book are to 1) provide general principles and conditions for making effective presentations, yet at the same time 2) provide a set of distinctions, a vocabulary and operational models which encourage awareness and flexibility in relation to managing a diversity of kinds of a) learning tasks, b) learning styles and c) learning contexts.

To accomplish these goals it will be necessary to:

1. Establish a framework for the process of learning, from the point of view of the learner as well as the instructor.
2. Explore some principles and strategies related to the learning process and instructional methodology.
3. Develop strategies to manage the mix of tasks and relational features that arise in teaching contexts. Communication strategy relates to the tasks to be accomplished but it also must relate to the relationship between the individuals involved in the learning process.
4. Explore managing a diversity of learning styles; including not only thinking styles, but different kinds of motivations and attitudes about the learning as well.

Some of these activities are more cognitively oriented, because developing a communication strategy does involve conceptualizing and analyzing. Other activities will be highly interactive and involve practicing behaviorally by simulating learning contexts and enacting different skills and models in order to bring them to life. Presenting and learning involves activating the nervous system through actions as well as through language. Thus, it would be useful to get together with a group of others to study and practice the material in this book.

part one

Basic Principles of Effective Presenting

The 'Problem Space' of Effective Presenting

Basic Presentation Design

Exploring Different Representational Channels

Strategies for Designing Reference Experiences

Overview of Part One

Basic Principles of Effective Presenting

The purpose of Part One is to:

1. Provide the foundation for understanding of the learning and teaching process in general and the significance of communication and relational skills.
2. Explore and define key elements of learning a) in individuals, b) between individuals and c) in groups.
3. Develop a) vocabulary, b) concepts and c) models to support and manage different learning processes and learning styles.
4. Define and apply some specific principles and methods for enhancing effective presentations.

Part One is made up of four chapters:

Chapter 1 The Problem Space of Effective Presenting

Defines some key elements of effective presentations and assists the reader to 1) develop awareness of his or her own conscious and unconscious competence with respect to making presentations, and 2) to elicit and observe these processes in other individuals.

Chapter 2 Basic Presentation Design

Introduces a set of models and distinctions that will assist the reader to identify various levels of structure to his or her own presentation skills and style and to define principles related to designing effective presentations.

Chapter 3 Exploring Different Representational Channels

Provides a number of strategies and methods for representing concepts, ideas and information and explore the influence of using different representational channels during a presentation.

Chapter 4 Strategies for Designing Reference Experiences

Explores ways of transferring knowledge and skills from the presentation context to the learners' realities by linking or 'anchoring' cognitive maps to relevant reference experiences.

Assumptions

The material to be covered in Part one is based on a set of *assumptions* about learning and presenting:

Learning is a natural, ongoing process that has structure. This structure is defined by the interaction of cognitive maps and the reference experiences which give those maps practical meaning.

Learning and teaching is essentially a process of enriching cognitive maps of a particular concept, idea or task and then linking those maps to reference experiences in order to enhance the behavioral competence and flexibility one has in relation to achieving goals and responding to environmental constraints.

Conscious competence is primarily a function of one's cognitive map of a particular idea, concept or task. Unconscious competence is a function of the type and number of reference experiences one has in relation to a particular idea, concept or task.

There is a both a natural and rational cycle to the learning process. Natural learning processes center around the development of unconscious competence. Rational learning processes center around the development of conscious competence.

Understanding the structure of and relationships between cognitive maps and reference experiences makes it possible to model and develop techniques and methods that can pragmatically enhance both the conscious and unconscious.

One goal of an effective presentation is to help learners widen their perceptions and cognitive maps of the 'perceptual space' of a particular idea, concept or task, in terms of the mode of representation of the idea or task and their basic assumptions. Another is to create and enrich the links cognitive maps have to various types of reference experiences.

Chapter 1

The Problem Space of Effective Presenting

Sets the overall frames for defining and exploring effective presentation skills in reference to:
1) establishing cognitive maps
2) creating relevant reference experiences
3) developing awareness of one's own conscious and unconscious competence with respect to making presentations
4) eliciting and observing these processes in other individuals

- **Presentation Skills and Organizational Learning**

- **The Problem Space of Presenting in a Learning Context**

- **Increasing Presentation Skills**

Presentation Skills and Organizational Learning

At some point in our lives we are probably all called upon to make a presentation of some sort. It may be at school, a social function or for some professional purpose. In fact, the demands of the 'information age' make it increasingly necessary and likely that we will need to make presentations as part of our normal activities.

To make an effective presentation requires that we be able to communicate and relate to other people. These are very basic skills, yet they are not typically taught to us as part of our traditional classroom education or professional training. The purpose of this book is to provide some of the key practical communication and relational skills necessary to make effective presentations.

There are generally four different purposes for making a presentation:

1) to inform others
2) to entertain others
3) to teach others
4) to motivate others

The goal of *informing* others is to provide them with key information or knowledge generally in the form of some kind of cognitive 'map'. The goal of *entertaining* others is to create a positive experience for people or to put them into a positive 'state'. The goal of *teaching* others is to connect knowledge or information to the relevant reference experiences and behaviors they will need to put that knowledge or information into action. The goal of *motivating* others is to provide a context or incentive which gives meaning to knowledge, experiences or behaviors such that people will want to take action. Of course, many presentations involve a mixture of some or all of these purposes.

While the skills in this book are relevant for all types of presentations, the focus of the book is on people who must make presentations for professional reasons. In particular, it focuses on presentations to be made for teaching and training purposes, i.e., those related to organizational learning. While this obviously includes professional trainers and teachers, it also includes managers, consultants and others who need to share knowledge and information.

Part of the mission of this book is to support the development of those organizations who wish to become 'learning organizations'.

The Emergence of the 'Learning Organization'

In order to address the accelerating changes in technology and society a new appreciation and concept of the role of organizational learning has emerged. Accelerating advances in management, technology and business methods have made it clear that the ability to learn, on both an individual and organizational level, is an ongoing necessity if organizations are to survive and succeed. Companies and other social systems have begun to realize that effective learning must be an incremental, goal-oriented process that has a structure, and that meeting the ongoing learning needs of a complex system requires organization and constant effort to maintain. This realization has lead to the rise in recent years of the concept of the 'learning organization'.

An effective learning organization is one that supports the process of learning in all of its dimensions - one that encourages *learning to learn*. This requires a basic valuing and understanding of the learning process. An effective learning organization needs to support not only learners and teachers but anyone who is involved in learning contexts within an organization.

According to Peter Senge (1990), there are five 'disciplines' which need to be practiced by everyone in an organization in order for it to truly become a 'learning organization':

1. Awareness and examination of mental maps and assumptions
2. Attaining self mastery
3. Developing vision
4. Team learning
5. Systemic thinking

The presentation skills covered in this book are designed to address and facilitate each of these 'disciplines'.

Summary of Presentation Skills and Organizational Learning

General Purposes for Making a Presentation

- **To inform**
  provide others with key information or knowledge

- **To entertain**
  create a positive experience for people or to put them into a positive 'state'

- **To teach**
  connect knowledge or information to the relevant reference experiences and behaviors

- **To motivate**
  provide a context or incentive which gives meaning to knowledge, experiences or behaviors

The focus of the book is on presentations to be made for teaching and training purposes, i.e., those related to organizational learning.

Key Points

There are generally four different purposes for making a presentation: 1) to inform others, 2) to entertain others, 3) to teach others and 4) to motivate others. Presentations involve a mixture of some or all of these purposes.

Summary of Presentation Skills and Organizational Learning
(continued)

> ## Senge's 5 Disciplines of a Learning Organization
>
> **1. Awareness and examination of mental maps and assumptions**
>
> **2. Attaining self-mastery**
>
> **3. Developing vision**
>
> **4. Team learning**
>
> **5. Systemic thinking**

Key Points

An effective learning organization is one that supports the process of learning in all of its dimensions - one that encourages *learning to learn*. Some key characteristics of learning organizations have been defined as those which:

1. help individuals to develop and apply basic systems thinking and problem solving skills
2. assist individuals in learning about their mental maps, assumptions and cognitive strategies in order to develop personal mastery
3. enhance team learning and coordination

The Problem Space of Presenting in a Learning Context

In a learning context, an effective presentation involves the interaction of a presenter, the audience or learners, the materials to be learned, the tools to support the material, and the task.

Thus, the basic 'problem space' of presenting involves the relationship between:

1) the presenter

2) the audience (or learners)

3) the material to be presented and learned

4) the tools and communication channels available to support the presentation of the material

5) the context in which the presentation is taking place

Communication and Relational Skills

Communication and relational skills relate to managing the interaction between the presenter and the audience in order to achieve the desired goals of the presentation - both the goals of the presenter and the goals of the learners. Relational skills most often have to do with managing one's role. Communication skills most often have to do with managing tasks. It is important to have a good mix of task and relational skills.

Communication involves the sending of messages back and forth between people who alternate between being 'senders' and 'receivers'. In a presentation context the presenter is primarily in the role of a 'sender' and the audience members are 'receivers'. In addition to managing the ongoing relationship with the audience, an effective presenter must also select, and in some cases design, the materials to be presented and the tools to support the delivery of the material. Managing the problem space of presenting, then, involves the skills to first assess the audience and then determine the appropriate information and channel of communication to present the information effectively. This requires that presenter be able to factor in a) the goals and motivations of the audience, b) their learning styles and c) their working reality.

The emotional and physical state of the people involved and their role relationships (status) are an important influence on how messages are sent and interpreted. Another important skill of a presenter is the ability to determine which state is most appropriate for the presenter to be in relation to the state of the audience (i.e., enthusiastic, calm, humorous, etc.) and have the ability to achieve and maintain that state. If an audience is cautious and the presenter is too enthusiastic, for example, there may be a lack of rapport that can lead to friction between presenter and audience.

Managing Diversity

A key issue in making an effective presentation is how to manage diversity. An effective presenter not only needs to present a diversity of contents and topics, but also needs to effectively interact with people from a diversity of cultures and professional backgrounds. This requires a focus on the process aspects of teaching and learning.

In many presentation contexts there are aspects of the learners' culture and personal or professional realities with which the presenter will not be familiar. At a process level, the presenter will need to encourage and help the learners to make the refinements and changes that are necessary to adapt specific content and skills to the learners' professional realities. Thus, an effective communication strategy requires creativity, knowledge about belief systems and the dynamics of groups, as well as new technologies and instruments for presenting and facilitating the process of continuous self-learning.

Communication and relational skills are made up of other cognitive and behavioral subskills. Effective communication and relational skills involve:

1) an understanding of people's subjective experiences

2) a set of principles and distinctions to recognize patterns in people's behavior and thinking styles

3) a set of operational skills and techniques that influence people's behavior and thought patterns

Different Types of Learning and Learning Styles

Teaching obviously relates to learning. And the effectiveness of a teacher improves to the degree that he or she is able to support the learning process of the learners. Different people learn in different ways. A presenter needs a set of distinctions and a vocabulary with which to identify different kinds of learning and presentation styles. An effective communication strategy facilitates different learning styles, and thus reaches a wider number of learners.

On another level, all learning shares some very fundamental and basic principles. Even though there are different types of learning and learning styles, there are features which remain constant about learning and managing the learning process, regardless of the context, the culture or the task. Being an effective presenter involves acknowledging and operating from that which is common to all learning, but then having the models, the discriminations and the flexibility to be able to adapt to different kinds of learning styles and learning contexts.

The Purpose of Communication and Relational Skills

Communication and relational skills support group and team learning by facilitating communication and understanding between people to help them more effectively accomplish their tasks. These skills are a function of how a presenter uses verbal messages (both spoken and written) and non-verbal messages (ranging from visual aids to variations of his or her own voice tone and gestures) in order to:

1. Facilitate understanding

2. Address different learning styles

3. Stimulate effective learning processes

4. Encourage participation and effective performance

Summary of The Problem Space of Presenting in a Learning Context

The 'Problem Space' of Presenting

- Type of Audience

- 'State' and 'Status' of Presenter

- Information to be Delivered

- Representational Channels

Key Points

The basic problem space of presenting relates to managing the interaction between the presenter and the audience in order to achieve the desired goals of the presentation.

In addition to managing the ongoing relationship with the audience, an effective presenter must also select and in some cases design the materials to be presented and the tools to support the delivery of the material, taking into account a) the motivation of the audience, b) their learning styles and c) their working reality.

Summary of The Problem Space of Presenting in a Learning Context (continued)

Communication and relational skills for presentations have to do with "how" we use verbal and non-verbal messages in order to:

- stimulate learning processes

- address different types of learning styles

- facilitate understanding

- encourage participation and effective performance

Key Points

Effective communication and relational skills involve an 1) understanding of people's subjective experiences, 2) a set of principles and distinctions to recognize patterns in people's behavior and thinking styles, 3) a set of operational skills and techniques that influence people's behavior and thought patterns.

Increasing Presentation Skills

Knowing about the structure of learning and presenting opens the possibility of enhancing one's presentation abilities to make oneself more effective. There are three key processes involved in enhancing one's presentation skills.

The first one is *"adding."* One way to enhance is to add. Adding has to do with what other processes or strategies can be added to the process that is currently being used. You could ask, "What could I add to what already exists, that is already working?" What could you add to your presentation skills to make you more effective?

The second process is *"transferring."* Transferring has to do with which patterns of a presentation that is effective in one context can be transferred to another context. There might be some aspect of a presentation that was effective in one context that, on a process level, might have value in other contexts. Thus, you might be able to transfer elements of an effective communication strategy from one context to another. Which patterns of your presentation could you transfer most easily to other contexts in which you would like to improve your presentation ability?

The third process for increasing one's presentation ability is *"coordinating."* Coordinating has to do with how different kinds of communication strategies, cognitive patterns and thinking styles can be coordinated between oneself and others. In this case the question would be, "How might I coordinate my presentation style with learning styles of others so that they're complementary instead of conflicting?" For example, a presenter might coordinate the channel of communication with the thinking styles of the audience. How could you improve the coordination of your presentation style with different styles of learning?

In the coming chapters we will be exploring each one of these ways of enhancing presentations in more detail.

Exercise 1 - Exploring Effective Presentation Skills

The purpose of this exercise is to experientially explore some basic elements of the personal experience of making a presentation. Its purpose is to bring out some principles of effective presentations and to enlighten you about some aspects of your own personal style of presentation through a concrete reference experience.

Part I

There are two roles in the exercise; a 'presenter' and an 'audience'. The 'presenter' is to choose a simple topic relating to effective communication and make a presentation. The group members are to observe the presentation and notice if there are patterns and consistencies of language and behavior relating to the presenter's style.

Instructions for the 'Presenter'

Your task is to choose a simple topic and make a short presentation. Identify a simple presentation topic relating to effective communication and take 5 minutes to present it to the group.

While you are presenting, see if you can begin to develop a 'meta cognition' (an introspective awareness) of your own processes and strategies - especially in terms of how you use language and representational channels. Try to experience the impact of language and the representational channels on your audience. In the back of your mind, start paying attention to what sorts of skills you utilize. How do you present a concept? How do you know that you are finished? What satisfies you that you've presented enough?

Even though the content of the exercise may be insignificant, the presentation skills used to communicate it may have similarities to other contexts which may be very relevant.

Instructions for the 'Observers'

While the 'presenter' is making the presentation, the group members will observe and notice what key verbal and behavioral patterns are demonstrated by the presenter. Observers should be aware that there is a difference between *observation* and *interpretation*. Observations are descriptions of actual behaviors, not inferences or projections about what those behaviors might mean.

Observers should focus on what is 'relevant' (i.e., what repeats, changes the most, or is the most exaggerated) in the language and physical behavior of the 'presenter'. Observers should also focus on key non-verbal cues such as body posture, facial expression, voice tone, and gestures.

After the 'presenter' has finished, the observers will share their observations of the presenter's behaviors. Then, switch roles and repeat the process with another presenter.

Part II

In the second stage of this exercise you will explore what kind of strategies, skills, principles and mental processes you used to make your presentation.

Instructions for Elicitation Process

Group members are to ask questions about their process during the presentation and compare their answers..

There are 3 basic questions to be considered.

The first one is, "What were the goals of your presentation?" "Was it a completely spontaneous process, or did you think about it?" "Did you just start improvising or did you have a clear idea of what you wanted to do?"

Question 2 is, "How did you know that you were finished?" "What satisfied you that you were finished or had presented 'enough'?" You might also explore whether you thought the presentation was effective. "Do you think the presentation that you made was very effective?" "Why? " Some people might have been pleased with their presentations while others might not. If so, why? Or why not? This has to do with the evidence for an effective presentation. "What specifically did you pay attention to as feedback during your presentation?"

The third question is, "What presentation skills did you use during your presentation?" "What representational channels did you employ to communicate to the group?" "What kinds of non-verbal communication did you use?"

These are the 3 basic questions. 1) What were your goals? 2) How did you know that you were finished? Were you happy with it? And then 3) What skills did you employ to make your presentation?

Remember, this is a general exploration; a discovery exercise. Its purpose is to discover some things about the presentation process and to begin to create reference experiences for key concepts we'll be using later on. The attitude to take towards this kind of exercise is that of being open to discover or explore; of being curious about learning something about your own process as well as your fellow presenter's processes. That's how you'll get the most out of it.

For instance, think about how you used the senses. What kind of representational channels were you employing? You can present concepts visually as well as verbally. Some presenters might have used a more visual process, or verbal or logical process. Some might have used a more physical approach. Some may have incorporated emotional reactions - eliciting a feeling about something. Of course, it is also possible to combine senses.

Also think about how you used your senses to observe your audience, to determine whether you were finished and whether you were being effective. Did you focus on what people said, how they looked or what they did?

Each person should take about 5 minutes apiece to answer these basic questions. Then switch to the next person. This should take about 20 minutes for the whole group. Group members should also observe for shared behavioral and observational skills.

The purpose of this part of the exercise is to recognize that communication strategies have a structure by experiencing the structure in your own strategy during a presentation. You should also begin to recognize some of the differences in styles and communication strategies depending on the types of goals for a presentation.

Discussion After the Elicitation

It is important to realize that different people have different styles and strategies, even for a simple task. Some of these differences relate to the kinds of goals one sets. A more physical strategy might be more effective for some kinds of presentations than a more verbal or visual approach.

Most of you probably noticed the distinction between your own conscious versus unconscious competences. You were probably not aware of everything you were doing while you were doing it. Many of you may have also discovered that there are a number of simultaneous processes to keep track of while making a presentation. Even in a very simple presentation there are combinations of different skills and styles.

Summary of Increasing Presentation Skills

Three Key Words to Increase One's Own Presentation Skills

1. **ADDING:**
   - What can one add to what already exists in order to improve it?

2. **TRANSFERRING:**
   - Are there presentation skills in one context that can be applied to another?

3. **COORDINATING:**
   - How can one coordinate one's own presentation style with the learning styles of others in order for them to be complementary (rather than conflicting)?

Key Points

There are three basic ways of enhancing presentation skills.

Adding: What other processes or strategies can be added to the process that is currently being used?

Transferring: Which patterns of a presentation that are effective in one context can be transferred to another context?

Coordinating: How can different kinds of communication strategies, cognitive patterns and thinking styles be coordinated within oneself or between oneself and others?

Summary of Increasing Presentation Skills (continued)

Exercise: Exploring Effective Presentation Skills

Phase 1

Each group member:
(a)   Identify a simple presentation topic.

(b)   Present it to a group of others for 5 minutes.

Phase 2

Compare your answers to the questions:
• What were your goals?

• How did you know you were 'done'? What made you satisfied that you had presented 'enough'? What kind of feedback did you pay most attention to?

• What presentation skills did you utilize to make your presentation?

Key Points

The steps of the exercise are to:
Make a simple presentation and trace the observational and behavioral skills you employed to enact it.

Recognize that communication strategies have a structure by experiencing the structure in your own presentation.

Observe others in the process of making presentations.

Notice that there are patterns of micro behavioral cues that provide feedback to a presenter.

Become aware of one's own conscious and unconscious competence with respect to making presentations.

Chapter 2

Basic Presentation Design

Introduces a set of models and distinctions that will assist the reader to identify various levels of structure to his or her own presentation skills and style and to define principles related to designing effective presentations.

- **Macro Structure of Experience and Learning: The T.O.T.E. Model**

- **Influence of Different Levels of Experience on Learning**

- **Defining the Basic Structure of a Presentation**

- **Designing an Effective Presentation**

Macro Structure of Experience and Learning: The T.O.T.E. Model

"The pursuance of future ends and the choice of means for their attainment are the mark and criterion of the presence of mentality in a phenomenon"
William James - ***Principles of Psychology***

Effective behavior is typically organized into a basic feedback loop called a T.O.T.E. (Miller, et al, 1960). The letters **T.O.T.E.** stand for *Test-Operate-Test-Exit*. The T.O.T.E. concept maintains that all mental and behavioral programs revolve around having a *fixed goal* and a *variable means to achieve that goal*. This model indicates that, as we think, we set goals in our mind (consciously or unconsciously) and develop a TEST for when that goal has been achieved. If that goal is not achieved, we OPERATE to change something or do something to get closer to our goal. When our TEST criteria have been satisfied, we then EXIT to the next step. So the function of any particular part of a behavioral program could be to (**T**)est information from the senses in order to check progress towards the goal or to (**O**)perate to change some part of the ongoing experience so that it can satisfy the (**T**)est and (**E**)xit to the next part of the program.

As you are trying to learn or present something, you're continually testing your progress. "How far am I?" "Is it going in the direction that I like?" "Is it useful?" "Is it innovative?" And, based upon the result of that test, you operate, you do something, and then you test again to check the effect of the operation. You test. You operate, trying to change something or make a step in the right direction. Then you test again; "Was the result of this operation effective?" Based on the result of this test, you either continue to operate or you exit; you're finished.

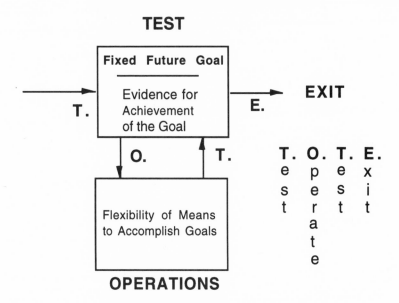

Figure 1. Diagram of Basic T.O.T.E. Feedback Loop

The test involves having a goal, an objective, and some sort of an evidence procedure for assessing progress toward the goal. In order to assess or to test, you have to have a direction and some evidence or evidence procedures that lets you know whether you are accomplishing the goal. To operate effectively, you need a range or a series of choices of activities from which you can select to accomplish this goal.

For example, one TEST for an effective presentation might be that an idea is made "clear". If the concept you have presented is not clear enough, you will OPERATE or go through a procedure to make the idea clearer or to come up with a better concept. Individuals will have different ways to TEST for something like "clarity" based on personal representational system preferences or proclivities. For instance, something like clarity may be determined on the basis of:

1) whether someone is able to see or visualize the concept
2) whether someone is able to do something physically or act on the basis of the concept

3) how someone feels emotionally about the concept

4) whether someone is able to repeat or verbalize the concept

These variations may make a big difference in the kind of result reached by the learning process and in the audience to whom it appeals.

A key characteristic of learning is the necessity of feedback. This is a characteristic that is demonstrated by all types of learning. There is no learning without feedback. Whether that feedback comes from the environment, from an instructor, from the consequences of the learners' actions, there must be feedback. The T.O.T.E. describes the essential features necessary to establish a self-correcting feedback loop. The T.O.T.E. states that an effective self-correcting feedback loop cycles between tests and operations until the desired goal is reached.

According to the T.O.T.E., the three key features of an effective feedback loop are 1) clear goals,   2) some kind of observable evidence for the achievement of that goal and 3) a flexibility of possible operations for achieving the goal. Effective trainers and presenters set goals, find evidences and then have a range of possible operations to deal with different contexts, different learning styles, and different kinds of unexpected situations. The goal always remains fixed, but the operations must have some degree of flexibility to account for variations in learners and learning contexts.

The T.O.T.E. is the fundamental framework for effective communication strategy, instructional methodology and essentially any kind of work breakdown structure.

The T.O.T.E. is a very basic process. Think of a child trying to walk. He has the goal of getting somewhere — say to a toy on a particular table or chair. He has evidence in terms of his relative distance from the toy, which can be seen and felt. He must then develop the skill and the flexibility necessary to get to his goal. Through many reiterations of testing and operating, his competency grows more and more. The child's goal, in this case, is fixed; get the toy. He has to have flexibility to accomplish that goal based on the potential flexibility and uncertainty within the system through which he is trying to move. If somebody moves the table or chair the toy is on, he has to readjust his operations. If he decided to fix his activity and just take a certain number of steps, he might reach his goal and he might not.

Consider the process of training. If you have a specific training goal, you have to vary the way that you do that training depending on the type of people in the training and the spontaneous situations that develop. If you fix a particular training procedure and stick to it no matter what happens, then you get variable results. You get a statistical distribution of success.

Of course, sometimes you want to produce varying results. In fact, some presenters, when they were doing the exercise, may not have even had a goal. They may have just started a process and noticed what happened. That's one form of presentation style.

Another presentation style would involve specifying a goal and then entering into a feedback loop with the audience, exploring the ways in which to accomplish that specific goal.

In either case, the T.O.T.E. defines the basic elements of the process. To have any kind of structured behavior, you need to have goals, evidence for reaching the goals and ways of accomplishing the goals. On a personal level, the way that we make these cognitive guiding maps and execute these programs is fundamentally through neurological processes like the senses. Whether it's for an individual or a group, goals could be set through language. They could be established visually, by drawing diagrams for example. The goal could also be set in terms of emotional responses or feelings or even a physical demonstration.

Then you have evidences and criteria for how well you're accomplishing your goal. Evidences especially are related to things that can be sensed and communicated. Evidence for the successful achievement of an objective will be seen, heard or felt in some concrete way. There is an important implication of this in terms of making presentations. Two people can have the same goal but a different evidence. Sometimes one person is using a visual picture as an evidence and the other person is using a feeling, and they might not find the same results even though they share similar objectives.

Summary of Macro Structure of Experience and Learning: The T.O.T.E. Model

The T.O.T.E. Model

Effective processes are structured around a basic 3-stage program or 'feedback loop':

1. An effective presentation is oriented to the achievement of goals.

2. It is important use tests/demonstrations to know whether one has moved towards or away from a goal, or accomplished it.

3. Given a 'negative' feedback, operations are performed as 'responses' to problems.

Key Points

According to the T.O.T.E. model, effective behavior is a function of a continual feedback loop between the assessment of goals and the enactment of operations to reach those goals.

For an effective performance, it is important to have clear fixed future goals, observable evidences indicating progress toward the goal and a flexibility of operations to reach the goal under changing conditions.

Key Points (continued)

In a typical communication T.O.T.E. for a presenter:

a) goals relate to influencing the thinking processes of learners in order to improve their understanding and/or increase motivation with respect to the topic.

b) evidences for the achievement of these goals comes through observations made of the audience's verbal and non-verbal responses.

c) operations are the actions of the presenter in the form of both verbal and non-verbal messages sent to the audience.

Influence of Different Levels of Experience on Learning

It is important to acknowledge that there are different levels of learning and different kinds of influences on learning. For instance, there's the *where* and the *when* of learning. This relates to environmental influences, such as space and time constraints, that might influence the learning process. For example, in the exercise for this chapter, presenters and learners had to operate in a limited time frame.

There's also the *what* related to learning. This refers to the kind of content and behavioral activities relating to the learning process. All of the presenters were given similar environmental constraints, but responded differently within these constraints. There was a wide variety of behavioral outputs within the similar environmental constraints.

But what accounts for these behavioral differences? Differences on a behavior level are triggered by differences in cognitive processes; that is, by differences in *how* one is thinking about something or mentally representing it. The how level of learning relates to the inner maps and the inner programs that trigger variations in content and behavior.

Learning also relates to beliefs and values. These determine the *why* of learning. "Why should a person bother learning something at all?" A person's degree of motivation will determine how much of his own inner resources he will mobilize. Motivation is what stimulates and activates the *hows* and the *whats* of our responses.

Finally, there's a *who* involved in learning. "Am I a good learner or presenter?" "Should somebody in my function or my role be a learner/teacher and in what types of contexts?" *Who* is supposed to learn/teach?

Review the exercise and notice which levels seemed to play a role in your presentation. Which levels most influenced your own personal experience of the exercise?

Levels of Learning

Any system of activity is a subsystem embedded inside of another system which is embedded inside of another system, and so on. This kind of relationship between systems produces different levels of learning, relative to the system in which you are operating.

People often talk about responding to things on different *"levels."* For instance, someone might say that some experience was negative on one level but positive on another level. In our brain structure, language, and perceptual systems there are natural hierarchies or levels of experience. The effect of each level is to organize and control the information on the level below it. Changing something on an upper level would necessarily change things on the lower levels; changing something on a lower level could but would not necessarily affect the upper levels. Anthropologist Gregory Bateson identified four basic levels of learning and change - each level more abstract than the level below it but each having a greater degree of impact on the individual.

These levels roughly correspond to:

a. Who I **A**m - *Identity*   Who?
b. My **B**elief system - *Values and Meanings*   Why?
c. My **C**apabilities - *Strategies and States*   How?
d. What I **D**o or have **D**one - *Specific Behaviors* What?
e. My **E**nvironment - *External Constraints*   Where? When?

The environment level involves the specific external conditions in which our behavior takes place. Behaviors without any inner map, plan or strategy to guide them, however, are like knee jerk reactions, habits or rituals. At the level of capability we are able to select, alter and adapt a class of behaviors to a wider set of external situations. At the level of beliefs and values we may encourage, inhibit or generalize a particular strategy, plan or way of thinking. Identity, of course, consolidates whole systems of beliefs and values into a sense of self. While each level becomes more abstracted from the specifics of behavior and sensory experience, it actually has more and more widespread effect on our behavior and experience.

* *Environmental factors* determine the external opportunities or constraints a person has to react to. Answer to the questions **where**? and **when**?

* *Behavior* is made up of the specific actions or reactions taken within the environment. Answer to the question **what**?

* *Capabilities* guide and give direction to behavioral actions through a mental map, plan or strategy. Answer to the question **how**?

* *Beliefs* and *values* provide the reinforcement (motivation and permission) that supports or denies capabilities. Answer to the question **why**?

* *Identity* factors determine overall purpose (mission) and shape beliefs and values through our sense of self. Answer to the question **who**?

Learning a multi-level process requires support from all these levels to be completely effective. Any level that is not aligned with the others can create an interference to the creative process. As an example, someone may have been able to do something new in a specific context (specific behavior) but not have a mental model or map that allows him or her to know how to continue doing new things or to innovative things in a different environment (capability). Even when someone is capable of learning, he or she may not value learning as an important or necessary function so they rarely use it. Even people who are able to learn and believe it is an important function do not always perceive themselves as "learners."

For instance, the following statements show how limits to learning could come from any one of the levels.

a. Identity: *"I am not a learner."*
b. Belief: *"Learning something new is difficult and time consuming."*
c. Capability: *"I don't know how to learn effectively."*
d. Behavior: *"I don't know what to do in this situation."*
e. Environment: *"There wasn't enough time to complete the lesson."*

Each of these processes involves a different level of organization and evaluation that will select, access and utilize the information on the level below it. In this way they form a hierarchy of "nested" T.O.T.E.s as shown in the following diagram.

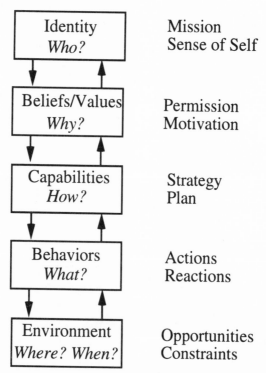

Figure 2. Diagram of 'Nested' Levels of Experience

Communication Strategy and Levels of Learning

It is important to take into account that there are different levels of learning and different levels of maps. We can build maps of our *environment* - the 'where', the 'when'. We can build maps of the *'what'*, of the *content* or the *behavior* to be brought into and enacted in that environment. We also build maps of the *'how'*, the plans, skills or strategies through which a behavior is enacted in a particular environment. One important assumption here is that maps of the 'how' are a different kind of map than the maps of the 'what' and that both are necessary in some way. There are also very important maps relating to the *'why'* of the learning task - what beliefs and values give it purpose, credibility or meaning. We may also have maps related to the *'who'* of learning - the role or identity of the learner.

To learn something effectively, learners need to know what to do. They need to know how to do it. They need to know why it is important. They need to know how it relates to who they are - their role. Different kinds of reference experiences might relate to different levels of the learning process. In one type of experience a person might get a reference for the 'what', but not necessarily 'why' or 'how'. A presenter is often working on multiple levels. It's the sequencing and the mix of these levels that is the essence of instructional methodology and communication strategies. Communication strategy has to do with issues such as "When does the presenter focus on the why?" If there is a resistance, is it because a learner doesn't know how to or doesn't want to? An effective communication strategy must then address how to deal with that particular issue.

In summary, a learning task may involve issues relating to 'wanting to learn', 'knowing how to learn' and getting the chance to learn. Wanting to learn often has to do with the 'desirability' of the outcome of learning or the why of the learning - the benefit of the learning. Knowing how to learn relates to the cognitive maps and the reference experiences that we create to install the process to be learned. And finally there's the chance to learn. This has to do with the context of the learning. The system in which the learning is being enacted, including the kind of support given to the learners - the where the when and the who in the environment. There are different ways in which trainers or presenters facilitate the chance to learn and the kind of relationships they assume with respect to learners.

The relative degree of emphasis on these different levels of issues and the sequence in which these issues are attended to are key elements of a communication strategy.

Summary of Influence of Different Levels of Experience on Learning

Levels of Learning

- *Environment* determines the external opportunities or constraints a person has to react to.
  Relates to the *where* and *when* of learning.

- *Behaviors* are the specific actions or reactions made by a person within the environment.
  Relates to the *what* of learning.

- *Capabilities* guide and give direction to behavioral actions through a mental map, plan or strategy.
  Relates to the *how* of learning.

- *Beliefs* and *values* provide the reinforcement (motivation and permission) that supports or inhibits capabilities.
  Relates to the *why* of learning.

- *Identity* involves a person's role, mission and/or sense of self.
  Relates to the *who* of learning.

Key Points

There are different levels of processes that influence learning and other human activities:

1) environmental processes determine the where and when of learning.

Key Points (continued)

2) it is through behavioral processes that the what of learning is manifested in the environment.
3) behavioral actions and responses derive from how one thinks - one's internal maps, strategies and mental capabilities.
4) one's approach to learning is influenced and directed by processes relating to beliefs and values which determine why one is learning something to begin with.
5) self referential processes relating to one's perception of who one is in relation to one's personal identity and role determine which kinds of beliefs and values will be selected and implemented.

Defining the Basic Structure of a Presentation

The Three Qualities of Successful Communicators

From observations of successful communicators in many different fields, three qualities have been found to be universal to every good communicator:

1) Good communicators continually set explicit and verifiable outcomes or goals.

2) Good communicators have the sensory awareness and observational skill to provide them with feedback about their progress toward their outcomes.

3) Good communicators have flexibility of behavior and continually change and adjust their communication to achieve their outcomes. If one approach isn't working, they have the flexibility to easily switch to another.

These qualities are related to the elements of the T.O.T.E. What are the goals that an effective performer has? What are the evidences that an effective performer uses to access progress toward his or her goals? What sort of range of activities or operations does an effective performer have available to accomplish his or her goals? What does an effective performer do when an operation or action doesn't work? Competence and excellence are not necessarily about being correct the first time. Competence often has to do with adapting to problems introduced by the environment or other parts of the system.

It is said that you don't really start managing until you run into a problem or a resistance. Until then, you're just giving instructions. It's not until there's a problem that you actually have to "manage." It is said that you don't really start selling until you run into a problem or a resistance.

Until then, you're just taking orders. It is said that you don't really start teaching until you run into a problem or a resistance. Until then, you're just giving information. How you respond to difficulties is an essential element to an effective presentation.

The Basic Structure of an Effective Presentation

Thus, the first step in designing a presentation is to define goals. There should be parallel goals established in terms of both task and relationship; and goals in terms of establishing cognitive maps versus reference experiences. Goals may be established in relation to developing conscious versus unveiling unconscious competence. For example, sometimes the presenter may want learners to experience something without any cognitive understanding in order to discover a principle or develop an unconscious competence. Because sometimes the awareness of what one is 'supposed' to learn can interfere with or get in the way of the actual learning experience. Thus, a presenter might specifically design a task such that the audience learns something that they don't know that they've learned until afterward.

So there are different types of goals to manage, different evidences related to the different goals, and a range of operations for reaching those goals. Learning goals should be specified in terms of the objectives for both the learner and the presenter. A presenter's goal, for example, should not be to simply 'deliver the required material'. It should also be to create strong learning experiences for the learners. The primary observable evidence for the achievement of goals in a training situation is the behavior of the learners. This evidence will occur not only in terms of their verbal responses to questions, but also in their non-verbal reactions and interactions with each other. The primary types of operations in the training environment relate to the interactions between the instructor and the learner, the learners and learning instruments and the learners with one another.

These parts of the T.O.T.E. are the core pieces of effective presentation design. Communication strategy has to do with how these basic feedback loops become sequenced with respect to task, relationship, cognitive maps and reference experiences. That is how the specifics of these core feedback loops become defined. The basic elements of communication involve people sending messages to one another through various media. People alternate between different positions in the feedback loop of sender and receiver. The content of a message is generally accompanied by higher level 'metamessages' (often non-verbal) that give emphasis or provide cues for how to interpret the message. The various media through which a message can be sent have different constraints and strengths which influence how the message is sent and received.

Summary of Defining the Basic Structure of a Presentation

Defining the Basic Structure of a Presentation

- Setting Learning Goals

- Establishing Evidence Procedures

- Defining Operations

- Responding to Problems

Key Points

There are different general types of presentation skills related to the different elements of the T.O.T.E.

Establishing and communicating goals

Defining and communicating evidence procedures

Establishing and communicating operations

Responding to problems and interferences

Designing an Effective Presentation

Later in this section, there is a questionnaire for defining a T.O.T.E. for making a presentation. The questionnaire relates to a context in which you will be making a presentation. It poses a set of questions relating to goals, evidences and operations as a self-modeling exercise.

The first question asks for a brief description of a context in which you will be presenting. Choose something that's relevant to you personally and to your professional reality.

The second question is, "What are the goals or objectives that you're attempting to accomplish through the presentation in that context?" Effective performance is triggered and mobilized by goals, and these goals might be on any number of levels. They might be on a *why* level or a *how* level or a *what* level. Rather than try to consciously figure out at what level your goals are at this point, just answer the question out of your own intuition for now.

Question 3 asks, "What will you use as evidence to know if you are accomplishing these goals?" These don't have to be extremely detailed answers. But you are going to be sharing this information with other group members. So you need to be able to describe it in enough detail that somebody else could understand what you mean.

Question 4 is, "What will you do in order to get to your goals? What kinds of steps or activities will you go through to present the material?" You might want to think in terms of the specific cognitive and behavioral processes you engage in the context you have identified.

Finally, Question 5 asks, "If you experience unexpected problems or difficulties, what is your reaction?" How do you respond to problems? What kind of actions do you take to correct problem situations that arise in this context?

This set of questions will give you an interesting insight into the elements that make up a personally effective performance. Even if you've presented in this context many times, you may discover some additional insights about your process by organizing your experience of it into these kinds of chunks.

To model a T.O.T.E. relating to a particular event, it is important to be able to think about the structure of the process "as if" you were living the experience. Your goal is to try to put down as much of what it would be like if you're actually engaged in the activity. At the same time, realize that you may also have to be doing a fair amount of guessing in anticipation. Since you will be answering these questions from imagination as much as memory, you may have never thought about some of these things before. So you might have to make a decision about what your experience would most likely be.

It should take approximately 10 minutes to fill out the questionnaire.

EXERCISE 2
Designing an Effective Presentation

Take a few moments and answer the following questions as completely as you can.

1. What is a context in which you will be making a presentation?

2. What are the goals or objectives that you are attempting to accomplish through the presentation in this context?

3. What will you use as evidence to know if you are accomplishing those goals?

4. What will you do to get to the goals - what are some specific steps and activities that you will use to achieve your goals in this context?

5. What problems or difficulties in achieving your goals in this context could arise? What will be your response to them? What specific activities or steps will you take to correct them?

Summary of Designing an Effective Presentation

Instructions to Fill in the T.O.T.E. Questionnaire

Identify a context in which you will be making a presentation:

Put yourself into the experience 'as if it were now.'

1. What goal/aim are you trying to achieve?

2. What evidences show that you are achieving or have achieved your goals/aims?

3. What do you do (which operations can help) in order to reach your goals?

4. With respect to a problem/uncertainty, what do you do to correct the direction of your actions?

Key Points

You can enhance your own communication strategy by specifying your T.O.T.E. for an event in which you will need to be able to present effectively.

To define a T.O.T.E. relating to a future event, it is important to be able to think about the structure of the process "as if" you were reliving the experience.

Chapter 3

Exploring Different Representational Channels

Provides a number of strategies and methods for representing concepts, ideas and information and explores the influence of using different representational channels during a presentation.

- **Representing Concepts and Ideas**

- **Other Types of Representational Strategies**

- **Creating Multiple Perspectives**

Representing Concepts and Ideas

One of the essential processes around which a presenter's activity revolves is the sending of verbal and non-verbal messages that serve the purpose of either communicating cognitive maps or creating reference experiences for the audience. All messages must be transmitted through some kind of medium. In presentation situations, the 'medium' through which messages are sent is made of:

1) the channel of communication

2) the context of the communication

3) the cultural framework surrounding the communication.

Channels of communication are related to the different sensory modalities by which a message may be represented. The context and cultural framework surrounding the communication relate to the types of assumptions and inferences which will be used to give meaning to the communication.

Representational Channels

Our abilities to learn and communicate come from our ability to make maps in our minds. We build our mental maps out of information from the five senses or *'representational systems': sight, sound, feeling, taste,* and *smell.* Our senses constitute the form or structure of thinking as opposed to its content. Every thought that you have, regardless of its content, is going to be a function of pictures, sound, feelings, smells or tastes, and how those representations relate to one another. We are constantly linking together sensory representations to build and update our maps of reality. We make these maps based on feedback from our sensory experience.

"Representational channels" relate to the senses and the type of sensory modality or representation a person is employing for a particular step in his or her communication or learning strategy. When someone is speaking out loud he or she is using a verbal channel of external representation. A more visual or symbolic form of external representation would involve drawing or displaying symbols and diagrams - when people think they might think in internal images or internally dialog with themselves.

The basic types of representational channels involved in making presentations are:

Verbal

Written

Pictorial

Physical

Check out the way you use these different representational channels internally and externally while you are presenting. For example, when you are setting goals, are the goals represented visually? Are they represented as actions, physically? Are they represented verbally? Perhaps they are represented simply as a kind of feeling.

Similarly, you might check whether the evidence you are using to know if you are accomplishing your goals is verbal, visual, emotional or physical?

When you present do you tend to be primarily verbal? Or do you also use pictures and imagery, or physically act out ideas by giving 'micro demonstrations'? Perhaps you have a clear preference for one of these representational channels.

It is also possible to use several types of representations or representational channels when presenting. For example, goals on a task level might be represented in terms of a picture or image of the desired result, but goals on a relational level might be represented verbally or emotionally. Certain ideas or concepts may be represented in terms of multiple senses such as feelings and imagery.

Which senses an individual uses to cognitively represent information, such as desired future events and potential consequences, is not simply a trivial detail. For example, some people run into problems accomplishing tasks because they have great visions but no comprehension of the feelings of effort that it might take to accomplish the vision, or no realization of the logical sequence of activities leading to the goal.

Representational Channels and Learning Styles

The notion of 'learning style' is basically a recognition, or an acknowledgment that people learn in different ways. Different people develop their sensory capabilities to different degrees. Some people are naturally very visual. Some people have a very difficult time forming visual images, or thinking visually at all. Some people are more verbal, and they can speak and articulate experiences very easily, and other people struggle with words. Words confuse them. And some people are very feeling-oriented, and learn by doing. A presenter needs to address the fact that people have different strengths.

A major part of communication strategy is directed not only at what the learner should learn, but who the learner is and how the trainer or presenter can in some way take that more into account. Effective communication involves the selection, sequencing and mix of which channels will be used to transmit which messages and the meaning of the various channels within the cultural framework in which it is being sent.

Influences of Different Representational Channels

Representational channels are an important dimension of a presenter's communication strategy. Different representational channels and verbal patterns direct the cognitive processes of group members in different ways and influence their perceptions of a group's role relations. For instance, writing is a simple way of encouraging consensus, because once something is out on a board the person who proposed it is not so intimately associated with the idea anymore. Externalizing an idea allows you to separate the *what* from the *who*.

Different modalities of representation have different strengths. The verbal mode of representation, for instance, has a lot of strengths in terms of how information is sequenced with respect to logical dependencies. The visual channel is often the best way to synthesize information into a whole or 'gestalt'. Acting out an idea or concept physically brings out its concrete aspects.

It is dangerous to automatically assume that others have the same thinking style as our own. Sometimes a person is not used to visualizing even though people are talking about things that require the ability to remember or fantasize visually. At other times a person might tend to focus too much on a particular image that has become imprinted in his or her mind. It stands out because it's unique or it's the only one that person has been exposed to. In challenging or stressful situations, people often revert to their most familiar representational channel.

We often make assumptions that others have the same cognitive capabilities that we do. But this most often is not the case. In communicating with others, matching their channel of representation is an important method of establishing rapport and insuring that they will understand a communication.

Learning can be enhanced by either strengthening somebody's weakness or utilizing their strengths. If somebody does not typically use visualization, encouraging them to think in terms of pictures could be very useful for them. If somebody is good at visualizing, emphasizing and enriching the use of that capability can also increase learning abilities in certain situations.

Emphasizing different channels of communication and representation can lead people into different kinds of thinking styles. For example, the visual channel helps to stimulate imaginative thinking. The verbal channel is often most effective for logical or critical thinking. Focusing on physical channels influences people toward an action orientation.

In summary, representational channels may be enhanced to increase learning in a number of ways:

1) matching the channel that is most used and valued by the type of learners (appealing to a strength)
2) using a channel that is not often used to stimulate new ways of thinking or perceiving (strengthening a weakness)
3) emphasizing the representational channel most appropriate or most suited to a particular cognitive process or type of learning task
4) enhancing overlaps or 'synesthesia' between different representational channels

Summary of Representing Concepts and Ideas

Influence of Representational Channels

Different channels of communication and representation have different uses and different strengths.
- The verbal channel helps put ideas in sequence.
- The visual channel is more useful to synthesize the elements of an idea.
- The kinesthetic channel helps make ideas more concrete.

Using the same channel as another person helps rapport and communication.

People can be lead to different types of thinking styles by emphasizing different representational modes.
- Logical/verbal for critical thinking
- Visual for imaginative thinking
- Physical for action orientation

Key Points

Different channels of communication and representation have different uses and strengths.

In communicating with others, matching the channel of representation is an important method of establishing rapport.

Key Points (continued)

Representational channels may be used to enhance learning in a number of ways: 1) enrich the channel that is most used and valued (enhancing a strength), 2) use a channel that is not often used to find a new way of thinking or perceiving (strengthening a weakness), 3) emphasize the representational channel most appropriate or most suited to a particular cognitive process or type of creativity, 4) enhance overlaps or 'synesthesia' between different representational channels.

Other Types of Representational Strategies

Once a concept or idea has been defined, the perceptual space that relates to the idea or concept can be explored by adding new elements to the existing map of the idea or concept or by changing that map in some way. There are several general processes which can be used to enrich the representation of concepts and ideas, and to improve and enhance learning and thinking ability. Each of them involves the process of representing something in a different way:

1) Using metaphorical or symbolic representations.

2) Changing representational channels.

3) Creating multi sensory maps.

One of the most basic communication strategies is that of representing one thing as something in a different way, either in symbolic representation or as a metaphor. Metaphors are a special form of language that give meaning to other messages and make links with deeper structures within people.

Rather than be secondary to reality, metaphors often provide the framework through which actual events and information is given meaning.

Another element of a communication strategy is changing the representational channel through which you are perceiving or mapping a concept or idea - such as changing from a verbal channel to a visual channel by drawing, or from visual to physical by acting something out, etc.

Another very basic aspect of communication strategy is using multiple channels of representation - as in a multimedia presentation.

In summary, there are three basic ways to enrich the representation of a concept or idea: 1) metaphor and symbolism, 2) changing representational channels, and 3) synthesizing channels of representation.

In general, the more richly a person is able to use his or her representational systems, the greater the number of connections will be stimulated or perceived.

Metaphors

Metaphor is probably the most fundamental form of lateral thinking strategy. We often think of metaphors as being simply 'illustrations' of reality, but in many ways our perceptions of reality are influenced by the deeper metaphors we 'live by'. That is, we often organize reality according to metaphors instead of the other way around. Metaphors offer simple but very highly encoded representations of fundamental relationships. They are often the most effective way of representing deeper level issues relating to values and identity. For example, thinking of an organization as a 'machine', a 'bee-hive' or a 'football team' can dramatically change the perception of the organization.

Metaphorical representation is a very common and powerful way of engaging new associations with respect to the understanding of an idea or concept. It is also a useful tool to transfer learning between different contexts. It stimulates a type of thinking that might lead to the level of abstraction necessary to transfer or apply particular learnings between contexts.

Making analogies between very different types of contexts can create new areas of perceptual space. For example, you might find that, although skiing is something one does by oneself and an office context has lots of other people, there still might be a kind of a metaphorical or analogical relevance between skiing and working in an office. You might make the analogy that avoiding trees and potholes while skiing is like dealing with the potential interferences created by people in the office.

Listening for micro metaphors within the idiomatic language used by a person (or common to a culture) can also serve to identify limiting assumptions or presuppositions and point the direction for new metaphors. For example, a person might talk about a communication problem in terms of an overly aggressive micro metaphor such as a "battle." If such a metaphor is shifted to something less aggressive like 'stepping on each other's toes," new perceptual spaces might be more easily found. Similarly, a leadership metaphor such as "holding the stick" could be shifted to something like "passing the baton."

Universals, Metaphors and Symbols as a Means to Transfer Learning

> *It is by metaphor that language grows.*
> *The lexicon of language...is a finite set of terms that by metaphor is able to stretch out over an infinite set of circumstances, even to creating new circumstances thereby.*
> *A theory is...a metaphor between a model and data. And understanding in science is the feeling of similarity between complicated data and a familiar model...understanding a thing is arriving at a familiarizing metaphor for it...*
> - **Julian Jaynes** *(The Origin of Consciousness in the Breakdown of the Bicameral Mind)*

There are two aspects relating to the transferability of a learning experience. One relates to the issue of analogy, or metaphor. The transferability of a learning experience is a function of the degree of the analogy between the representations and metaphors used in the presentation and the learner's working reality. To the extent that they are similar in the features that are relevant for the transfer, then one can be used as a reference experience for the other.

Analogy is a very powerful communication strategy because it stimulates learners to think, "How is this like that?"
"What can I take from what I already know as an analogy to
the new concept or idea?" For example, a presenter might
use a metaphor such as 'designing an apple' to illustrate a
concept or stimulate thinking in regard to 'designing an
engine'. On a process level there might be similarities between the two; but on an operational level there might be
aspects of designing the apple that don't transfer to the
operations of designing the engine. Often this kind of
analogy is valuable with respect to understanding, but when
it comes to actually operationalizing a behavior, then I might
have to use a different kind of simulation or representational
method.

'Universals' are especially important for making presentations. Universals are common metaphors or experiences that
a whole audience is able to recognize and relate to. A
universal would be shared experiences that everybody within
a group is likely to have had or observed. For example,
something like a 'child learning to walk' or 'preparing a
meal', etc. A question a presenter might want to ask himself
is, "How much can I connect what I'm trying to teach to
universal experiences?"

Some universals are more useful for understanding an
idea or concept, others help to transfer learnings from the
presentation environment to the audience's reality.

There are different levels of how universal a particular
experience is. In a particular culture, a concept may be
universal, but the behavioral skill might not be. To transfer
concept, something might be a very good metaphorical reference, but then to transfer the actual capability, the presenter
might need other forms of representations or reference experiences.

A third element that influences the transferability of a
learning experience has to do with the 'symbolic' aspect of
the experiences. Symbols and symbolic experiences are a
powerful tool for learning. Symbols are often associated with
and thus mobilize, deeper structures of experiences such as

beliefs and identity (e.g., a nation's flag, a company's logo or uniform).

A reference experience might have a symbolic value as well. 'Designing an apple' could also be a symbolic statement. In a way, it is more of a symbolic process than it is an actual process. Nobody does actually design an apple, but it symbolizes taking a particular approach to thinking about something.

Symbolic experiences often are internalized more deeply and transfer more widely than a specific piece of information or a specific example.

A role play, for example, is primarily thought of as a modality to practice a specific skill. But role plays also have a symbolic value. For example, in some role plays, even if people have never had the particular experience as it actually happened in the role play, it can be so symbolic of their reality, that it is actually a more powerful learning experience than simply practicing a behavioral procedure.

Symbolic experiences are often related to belief and values. They represent something in the culture as opposed to just a physical situation. Examples or analogies might also be symbolic as well as just instructive.

Cognitive Packages

Concepts, ideas and complete cognitive maps are communicated through a series of 'cognitive packages'. A 'cognitive package' is a 'chunk' of communication which serves to either build up a larger cognitive map or contribute to the creating of a reference experience. Typically, a more sophisticated cognitive package might be formed out of other simpler cognitive packages.

Cognitive packages are the concrete pieces that are graphic or verbal or somehow tangible, the kinds of messages you're trying to send in order to form the map of a concept or idea and connect it to reference experiences. For example, a transparency is a cognitive package. An example, or metaphor, is a cognitive package. An explanation is a cognitive package.   These examples are cognitive packages formed through different representational modalities.

The value of thinking of communication in terms of 'packages' is that you can then repackage them or resequence them according to what kind of representation is effective for what kind of learning process. The representational channel through which a cognitive package is sent has an important influence. A picture might help somebody visualize a whole system, but verbal instructions are effective for procedural information.   Physical actions help shape a person's actions more directly.

Influence of Different Kinds of Representations on Learning

A perceptual space is defined by the parts of a system of elements one considers to be relevant to the idea/concept. The way you represent a perceptual space will determine what kind of associations and connections are likely to be made. Different kinds of representations 'punctuate' a perceptual space in different ways and highlight different factors and relationships in that space. Different types of representations and representational channels also encourage different types of thinking processes. For instance, a critic is more likely to emerge in response to words than symbolic images.

Different forms of maps are more effective for representing information on different levels:

What —▶ words

How —▶ diagrams

Why —▶ symbols

Who —▶ metaphors

The influence of Assumptions on Communication

Context and culture are other aspects of the medium through which messages are communicated. Context and culture determine the kinds of assumptions and expectations an audience will apply to interpret the meaning of a communication.

In order to give meaning to a particular representation or experience, one must make *assumptions* about the perceptual space in which one is operating. Different assumptions influence the priority and relevance one gives to elements of the idea or experience.

Summary of Other Types of Representational Strategies

Some Other Types of Representational Strategies

- Metaphors

- Analogies

- Symbolic Representations

- Micro Demonstrations

Key Points

There are several general processes which can be used to improve and enhance learning. Each of them involves the process of representing information in different ways.

1) Metaphorical or symbolic diagrams
2) Changing representational systems
3) Creating multi sensory maps

In general, the more richly a person is able to use his or her representational systems, the greater the probability of effective learning.

Creating Multiple Perspectives

One powerful form of cooperative learning arises out of the fact that people have different maps of the world. The way that somebody else represents a particular idea or concept can automatically stimulate new perspectives and insight in other audiences.

The next exercise is designed to take advantage of this natural process of cooperative learning.

The exercise has to do with the influence of representational channels. It is to be done in a group of four in order to get enough of a range of diversity.

Each group member chooses an idea or concept that is important or challenging to present The group may decide to choose one particular topic to explore.

Group members are to determine which representational channel is typically used to communicate the idea/concept. Then, each is to come up with 2 other ways to represent the same idea/concept. For example, one might draw a symbolic or metaphoric picture of the idea/concept, or make a diagram or sketch. It is also possible to make a physical micro demonstration. What is important is that the idea or concept be represented in a new way through a different representational channel.

Each person makes his or her own representations individually without looking at the work of the others. So, each person makes 3 representations of the idea/concept he or she has chosen: the standard representation and two alternative representations in different representational channels. Then each group member presents the idea or concept to the others using the usual channel and the 2 new ones. Contrasting different maps and representations of an idea or concept is a way to enrich the perceptions of the idea/concept and create a fuller understanding.

This is an exercise on representing and widening the perception of an idea or concept.

After each person has presented the 3 alternative representations of the idea/concept, group members are to discuss what is different about the various ways of representing the idea/concept. The group is to determine what is effective about the new representations and what the strengths and weaknesses are of each form of representation for different learning styles and outcomes.

If all of the groups want to share a similar topic area in order to explore potential generalizations, they may choose a topic related to effective communication.

The presupposition of the exercise is that making external maps through different representational channels is an effective method to:

1) acknowledge the diversity of learning styles between people and

2) develop multiple perspectives of an idea or concept

Exercise 3: Creating Multiple Perspectives

Form a group of four. Each person will take a turn being the presenter.

1) Each group member picks an idea or concept that is important or challenging to present (or the group may choose to all use the same topic).

2) Each group member individually determines which representational channel is typically used to communicate the idea/concept.

3) Each group member individually comes up with 2 other ways to present the same idea/concept; such as pictorial, metaphorical, symbolic or through a microdemonstration.

4) One at a time, each group member individually presents the idea/concept to the group using the usual channel and the 2 new ones.

5) The group discusses the impact and effectiveness of the different modes of representation.

Following the discussion, the group rotates to the next presenter.

Chapter 4

Strategies for Designing Reference Experiences

Explores ways of transferring knowledge and skills from the presentation context to the learners' realities by linking or 'anchoring' cognitive maps to relevant reference experiences.

- **Basic Processes of Learning**

- **Types of Reference Experiences**

- **"Anchoring" Reference Experiences**

- **Establishing and Anchoring Reference Experiences**

Basic Processes of Learning

Cognitive Maps and Reference Experiences

In its most general sense, *learning* may be defined as adaptive changes in behavior as a result of experience. In general, this involves a process in which individuals change their behavior in order to change the result they are creating in their environment.

Individuals change their behavior through the establishment of personal reference experiences and cognitive maps. Even the simplest forms of animals and insects appear to form cognitive maps of their environment so that they are able to follow some kind of map drawn from experience that is not coming from their immediate external environment. A large part of learning, even in the simplest animals, is in the creation of cognitive models and cognitive maps.

However, we are probably all familiar with the problem of having cognitive knowledge without any experiential knowledge. In these situations we know 'about' something but are unable to act upon that knowledge or put it into practice. Another part of the learning process, then, has to do with facilitating behavioral performance in respect to cognitive maps and models. Effective performance has to do with enacting a model or connecting it with behavior or to personal experiences. Thus, the primary event in learning involves the connection of some kind of cognitive map to some kind of concrete reference experience. This is especially important in helping learners transfer learnings from the presentation context to their professional reality.

Unconscious competence or latent competence comes from the establishment of reference experiences. Conscious competence comes from the ability to code one's experiences. Coding is the establishment of a connection between a map, abstraction or label and personal reference experiences.

The basic skills of learning involve the ability to establish cognitive maps and reference experiences, and the ability to perceive the state of the environment so that the appropriate cognitive maps and reference experiences will be mobilized to produce the desired results within the context of the individual's current system.

The essential process of facilitating learning involves assisting learners in (a) the formation of an internal cognitive map and (b) the connection of that map to the appropriate reference experiences which give that map practical meaning in terms of external observations and behavioral results. The general activities of a presenter, in a learning context, are centered around delivering cognitive packages and creating reference experiences through some kind of learning activity.

> a. *Cognitive Packages*- define a particular perceptual 'space' to be established or opened. A specific *cognitive package* is a verbal or visual embodiment or manifestation of an idea or concept.

> b. *Learning Activities*- define the reference experiences needed to give the cognitive package practical meaning. The verbal labels and examples, and the visual symbols which make up cognitive packages, acquire practical meaning for a learner only through their connection to personal reference experiences. A *reference experience* is a) a personal memory, b) an ongoing observable behavioral demonstration or c) a constructed (imagined, fantasized) experience, on the part of the learner. The purpose of such experiences is to activate either existing unconscious competence or other already existing perceptions or abilities.

In essence, the activities of a presenter serve one of four purposes:

1. Deliver cognitive packages
2. Help widen the learner's perceptual maps
3. Activate reference experiences for cognitive packages
4. Connect reference experiences to cognitive maps

Accomplishing these objectives involves helping learners expand their perceptual maps of the material being covered by stimulating associations between cognitive material and the learners' general or professional reality. Thus, learners are continually engaged in a cycle moving from thinking to doing; from map to territory. An effective presentation is a function of the presenter's ability to use language and other cognitive processes to a) stimulate learning processes, b) represent ideas and concepts and c) help people perform tasks more effectively.

This leads to three basic areas of focus in designing a communication strategy. One is what kind of cognitive map to choose and how to assist people to develop that map in themselves. Two is what kind of reference experiences are most effective and appropriate to enact these cognitive maps. Three is how to form a connection between the two. That becomes the final act of learning - the so-called "ah ha!" experience. The recognition that "This map goes with that experience."

Regardless of the kind of learning in which one is engaged, in some way these three factors will be involved. Having 1) some cognitive models, 2) some experience, and 3) some connection between them. The richness or the robustness of that connection is very often the key to skilled performance.

The Learning Cycle

Another fundamental aspect of learning has to do with how reference experiences and maps become 'piled up' in order to produce the final learning experience. Experiential learning tends to occur in a cycle that involves several key phases. Competence comes from 'piling up' reference experiences through doing and acting. Conscious awareness comes from having cognitive maps and distinctions with which to label and 'understand' behaviors and experiences. A typical pathway in the learning process begins with 'unconscious incompetence'. The individual does not know the skill and, furthermore, does not know that he or she doesn't know. For instance, if you ask a four year old, "Can you drive your daddy's car?" the child might well reply, "Oh, sure, I can drive daddy's car." The child doesn't have the competence but is not aware that he or she doesn't have the competence. Often people are unconscious that there is even something to be competent about. A person who has never been exposed to computers has no real idea of what competencies are required.

The second phase of this path is often the most challenging. It occurs when the learner becomes consciously incompetent. And the reason I say this is the most challenging phase is that people often have strong emotional responses to 'not knowing'. For some learners understanding is connected to survival. If they don't know something, they're afraid. It would be like a child becoming afraid of cars when he begins to realize that he is not in fact competent with "daddy's car" and that cars are dangerous. The child perceives his incompetence as connected with danger. There is also a lot of negative social judgment associated with 'incompetence'.

Not everyone has a negative emotional response to this phase. Some people are excited by realizing that they have something new to learn. The difference between whether someone responds positively or negatively to this phase often relates to his or her self-perception. The reason one person could be excited by recognizing their incompetence and another becomes afraid may relate to their expectations of their own capabilities. If a learner becomes aware of something that she doesn't know, but believes she is a capable person, then she will most likely perceive the learning task as a challenge. If she believes she is not particularly capable, then the learning task will most likely be perceived as difficult and threatening. People's self-perceptions are sometimes a very relevant factor in their response to 'not knowing' or being assessed related to performance.

In terms of communication strategy, learners' responses to the 'conscious incompetence' phase is a very relevant thing to attend to and have some means of addressing. Somebody who has little belief in his or her own capabilities to learn might require more coaching or mentoring, whereas the person has the confidence in his or her capabilities to learn might simply need a little guidance. Types of emotional reactions to conscious incompetence might be related to specific individuals, a whole group or a culture of people. We might expect that, for example, people who work in a factory might have a sense of confidence in their competency in technical areas and doubts about their competency in conceptual areas. Managers might have the reverse set of expectations. By anticipating potential responses to conscious incompetence, a trainer can determine the kind of communication strategy and relational support that an individual or group is most likely to require.

Following the conscious incompetence phase is the process of attaining 'conscious competence'. When a person is learning to drive a car, the person consciously learns to check the mirrors, fasten the safety belt, shift gears, judge distances, remember the rules, etc. There is a certain amount of 'clumsiness' and 'self-consciousness' associated with this phase.

In the typical pathway, the learner finally ends up reaching the phase of 'unconscious competence'. The individual no longer needs to consciously think about what he or she is doing. After a person has driven an automobile long enough, the amount of conscious effort the individual needs to put in diminishes because the tasks and skills are performed as an unconscious competence. As reference experiences pile up, the need for explicit cognitive maps diminishes.

The cycle of moving through conscious incompetence and conscious competence in order to achieve unconscious competence is only one possible path. There are also many cases in which individuals move directly from unconscious incompetence to unconscious competence. They develop competency through experience but have no cognitive maps. They are competent but can't explain or describe anything about what they actually do. Their ability seems more like a talent than a learned skill. This is the basis for what is called 'latent learning' or 'insight learning'. In cases where learners are likely to have a high degree of unconscious competence, an effective communication strategy is to identify the kinds of latent capabilities the learners are most likely to have and help them become aware of what they are already doing.

For example, native speakers of a particular language do not consciously think about how they organize the grammar of their sentences as they speak, and yet they do it practically perfectly. That is an example of unconscious competence. On the other hand, if one wanted to be a linguist it would be important that one developed some kind of conscious competence in order to be effective. It is difficult to teach someone about the structure of a language without conscious competence; whereas one can use the language without being consciously aware of what one is doing. It's possible to be unconsciously competent with a language and not consciously competent. Native speakers of a language do not always get good scores on their grammar tests. Of course, the way that grammar is taught is not always conducive to leading learners to easily grasp it conceptually.

One of the primary challenges for a trainer or presenter is how to find ways to make conscious competence more accessible. It is possible to make and teach conceptual models that actually make it harder for people to recognize or develop competence because they are not organic or do not fit the learning styles of the learners.

As a summary, organizational learning occurs in two basic ways: a) through a 'natural' learning process and b) a 'rational' learning process. In a rational learning process, learners use tools and models to develop a conscious competence. In a natural learning process, learners focus on goals and move directly to unconscious competence, but have no models or tools to understand, transfer or manage the growth of their capabilities. Most institutionalized training tends to be a 'rational' learning process that emphasizes the development of conscious competence; although both natural and rational learning process are finalized in the development of unconscious competence.

Summary of Basic Processes of Learning

Basic Processes of Learning

• **Establishing Cognitive Maps**

• **Connecting Cognitive Maps to Reference Experiences**

Key Points

The basic process of learning involves the connection of cognitive maps to reference experiences.

In relation to the basic process of learning, the purpose of presentation is to:

1) Provide cognitive packages in the form of language, labels and symbols.

2) Help people form a cognitive map of the ideas and concepts to be learned.

3) Activate or create concrete reference experiences.

4) Facilitate the connection of cognitive packages and maps to the relevant reference experiences.

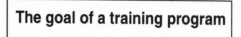

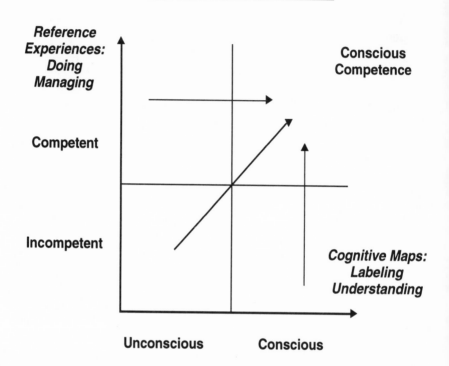

Key Points

Competence comes from 'piling up' reference experiences through doing and acting.

Conscious awareness comes from having cognitive maps and distinctions with which to label and 'understand' behaviors and experiences.

Organizational training tends to be a 'rational' learning process that emphasizes the development of conscious competence.

Types of Reference Experiences

A primary duty of presenters is delivering cognitive maps to people. When those maps are delivered without providing any reference experiences, then the trainer or presenter is just providing information. In other words, having a cognitive map without connecting it to reference experiences is simply information. The 'use' of the information comes as that map is connected to specific activities and generalized to other reference experiences. The evaluation as to how well learning has taken place is in reference to the richness and robustness of the connections between maps and reference experiences.

The task of the trainer or presenter is to deliver some kind of cognitive package, and then try to connect it to some kind of experiences that are initially generated in the context of the classroom. Then the question is, "Can the learner generalize the map to other experiences and contexts?"

Let's say we have a concept like "learning cycle." Someone can have a general understanding of that map, but then ask, "So what?" It needs to be connected to several reference examples that help to make it more concrete and meaningful. Once the map is connected to some experiences, learners will try to connect it to others themselves. And then they check whether it is an appropriate example with the instructor. The depth of learning on the part of the student comes by generating new examples, and connecting the concept to other experiences, then having a way of checking the validity of what they have generated and internalized.

There are different kinds of reference experiences. Giving an example of the learning cycle by describing the process of learning to play a musical instrument is a verbal example. A physical example comes from learners actually doing something. There are also visual examples in the form of demonstrations or illustrations.

During the learning process, the nervous system is making connections between one kind of map and another kind of map, and between maps and behaviors. Inside of a person, experiences are 'piling up' as interconnections are being established. A learner might have a reference experience for what a 'learning cycle' is, but not how to use it or why it's important.

A key consideration for a presenter is whether the reference experience he or she intends to activate is 1) a remembered experience - having people recall something from their past, 2) an ongoing experience - producing something in the moment, or 3) it's some sort of constructed or imagined scenario.

A scenario is a constructed experience. Questionnaires might cause people to access remembered experiences or imagine anticipated events. Demonstrations or simulations are to produce ongoing experience.

For example, in the context of this book the first exercise in which group members had to choose a topic and make a 5 minute presentation produced an ongoing reference experience. It was a concrete action unfolding in real time. The T.O.T.E. questionnaire required learners to imagine an anticipated presentation context. The exercise on creating cognitive packages involved a combination of memory, imagination and ongoing experiences. It initially involved access to a remembered experience. Then it required learners to act out an example with the group. Finally that example was used to point to future possibilities and alternatives.

The choice of type of reference experiences depends on the goals of the presentation and, to a certain degree, on the type of audience. For example, if a group does not have access to shared experiences and memories, then the presenter is either going to have to create something in the moment, or perhaps have to construct or imagine similar experiences.

The choice might also be influenced by the cognitive learning styles of the audience. How much imagination am I requiring from a group, versus what kind of memory? People vary in their ability to remember and imagine experiences.

Summary of Types of Reference Experiences

Types of Reference Experiences

- **Ongoing**
  external experience which is unfolding in real time

- **Remembered**
  recalled experiences from the past

- **Constructed**
  "as if" experiences that are constructed or imagined by the learner

Key Points

There are 3 basic types of reference experiences: 1) those relating to remembered past experiences, 2) ongoing experiences happening in the present environment and 3) imagined or constructed experiences (most often related to the future).

Different mixes of reference experiences are appropriate for different presentations depending on the goals of the presentation and the constraints of the presentation context.

'Anchoring' Reference Experiences

The process of 'anchoring' is a way to solidify and transfer learning experiences. 'Anchoring' involves establishing an association between an external cue or stimulus and an internal experience or state.   One analogy for anchoring is the example of Pavlov ringing the bell for his dogs. A lot of learning relates to conditioning, and conditioning relates to the kind of stimuli that becomes attached to reactions. An anchor is the kind of stimulus that becomes associated with a learning experience.   If you can anchor something in a classroom environment, you can then bring the anchor to the work environment as, minimally, an associative reminder of what was learned.

As an example of this, a group of learning psychologists did a research study with students in classrooms. They had students learn some kind of task in a certain classroom. Then they split the class in half and put one of the groups in a different room. Then they tested them. The ones who were in the same room where they had learned the material did better on the exams than the students who had been moved to a different room. Presumably this was because there were environmental cues that were associated with the material they had been learning.

We have probably all been in the situation of experiencing something that we wanted to remember, but when we got into a new environment where all the stimuli were so different, it was easier to forget. By developing the ability to use certain kinds of anchors, presenters can facilitate the generalization of learning in their audiences.   There will certainly be a greater possibility that learning will be transferred if one can also transfer certain stimuli.

There's another aspect to anchoring related to the fact that Pavlov's dogs had to be in a certain state for the bell to mean anything.   The dogs had to be hungry; then Pavlov could anchor the stimulus to the response. Similarly, there is an issue related to what state learners are in, in order to effectively establish an anchor. For instance, a transparency is a map, but it's also a stimulus. That is, it gives information, but it can also be a trigger for a reference experience. A presenter needs to know when to send a message or not to send a message. If people have a sudden insight - Aha! - and you turn on a transparency, it is going to be received in a different way and associated in a different way than if people are struggling with a concept.

Timing can be very important. It is important for a presenter to time the presentation of material in relation to the state of the audience. If the presenter has a cognitive package he or she wants to present, such as a key word or a visual map, he or she must wait for the moment that the 'iron gets hot'. When the presenter senses that there's a kind of a readiness, or a surge, or an openness in the group, at that moment he or she would introduce the concepts or show the key words. Because the point of anchoring is that a presenter is not just giving information, he or she is also providing stimuli that gets connected to the reference experiences of the audience. This is why stimuli that are symbolic are often more effective anchors.

The kinds of questions that a presenter needs to ask himself are, "When do I introduce this idea?" and "How strongly do I want people to experience it, or respond to it?" For example, if the presenter is stimulating a discussion, an issue might arise that is deeply related to beliefs and values that is strongly felt, especially by some people. In that moment, if the presenter puts information out, it becomes connected with that degree of interest, or that degree of involvement.

The point is that anchoring is not simply a mechanical matter of presenting cognitive maps and giving examples. There's also the issue of the state of commitment or interest of the audience, as well. Sometimes a presenter will want to let a discussion go on, not only because people are making logical connections, but because the state of the group is intensifying and you want to capture that moment. In other times, if the state of the group is diminishing, for whatever reason, the presenter might not want to anchor that state to certain topics or reference experiences.

Presenters may use anchors to reaccess states in themselves as well as in their audience. It is possible for a presenter to use a self-anchor to get into the state he or she desires to be in as a leader of a group. A self-anchor could be an internal image of something that, when thought about, automatically brings on that state; somebody one is close to, for instance. One could also make a self anchor through an example; talking about one's children, or some experience that has a lot of very deep associations.

Establishing an Anchor

One of the skills of effective presenters is being able to 'imprint' something by catching those moments when information will be associated with positive or powerful internal states. Pavlov found there were two ways of creating associations. One is through repetition, continual reference back to an association between a stimulus and a response. The other has to do with creating something that is very intense and specifically connected to a particular stimulus. People, for example, can remember something forever, if it's associated with something highly emotional or highly important. They don't need to repeat it over and over. The association is made immediately.

There are two aspects related to establishing an anchor for a group. One is the continued reinforcement of the anchor. Pavlov found that if he started ringing the bell and not giving the food, eventually the response to the bell would diminish and fail. For an anchor to last through time, for a long time, it has to be in some way reinforced. This is an important issue with respect to continual self-learning and tutoring after a presentation. In that case, what a presenter chooses as an anchor might be something that could be passed on to others. It is important to have a consistency of language and models.

The other aspect has to do with how rich the initial anchor is. If a presenter has a limited time, he or she will have less time for repetition. Then the presenter will have to try to intensify the impact of the information and the anchors. It is obviously more desirable to anchor learnings in the classroom or presentation environment, but anchoring negative situations is also an important part of learning. Creatures learn by both approaching positive rewards and avoiding punishments.

Anchoring is a very interactive skill, but a presenter should think of anchoring as he or she is preparing a presentation, as well. A presenter might want to consider what kinds of anchors could be used to solidify associations to particular information or experiences. It is best to choose stimuli for anchors that appear not only in the classroom but also in the audience's reality.

Which anchor one chooses is going to determine how that anchor can be used later on. Let's say a presenter is trying to get a group into a positive state for brainstorming, and has done a very nice job of eliciting a motivated state. The question will be, how could the presenter anchor that state so that he or she could get back to that same degree of motivation more quickly? One way is through particular behaviors of the presenter - a special eye contact, or facial expression, that could be used again later to trigger that state. Another way is to use something external as a means to draw the focus of the group - like pointing to a flip chart or referring to a transparency.

These are different types of anchors and they have different implications in relation to transferring information. Some presenters are very charismatic, and people anchor all of their learning to the presenter. But when the trainer isn't there, then the learnings begin to dissipate. Sometimes you can anchor a successful experience to the technique. Or you can anchor it to some kind of symbolic stimuli. Which you choose is an important strategic decision. People can say they were successful because a certain person was the leader, or they can say they were successful because they did the technique correctly, or because you understood.

In classroom and presentation contexts there are a number of natural anchors. Notebooks are anchors. Slogans can be an anchor. When people work together in a particular environment, they can become anchors for each other to transfer learnings from a course or presentation. When people see somebody they were with at a presentation, it can remind them of what they learned.

In summary, anchoring is a different level of process than coding that helps the transferring of knowledge that might not be transferable otherwise. It is an organic process that is used both in and outside of the classroom. Think of an athlete preparing for a contest.

As a personal example, when my wife and I were preparing for the birth of our second child, I was in the role of her coach. One of the challenges of being a coach during birth is that the experience is so intense that it's hard to transfer everything you know because the real situation is so different than the one in which you practice. You practice breathing and the various other techniques at home in a comfortable state, but when the reality happens it's a completely different situation that makes it difficult to remember all the techniques that you have practiced.

So, we decided to make an anchor. When my wife was in the state that she wanted to be able to maintain throughout this process, I asked her to make a symbol. What would symbolize this state? And she imagined a nautilus shell. It's like a snail shell that has a big opening on the bottom, so it has a nice symbolic value. So, I went and actually bought one of these shells. Then during all our practice sessions, she would focus her eyes on the shell. Then we brought the shell into the hospital during the actual childbirth process, and the shell became an ongoing trigger to help generalize the desired state to the actual birthing process. It was quite effective for both of us.

Summary of Anchoring' Reference Experiences

'Anchoring'

Anchors employ the process of association to:

- **focus awareness**

- **reaccess cognitive knowledge and internal states**

- **connect experiences together in order to**
  enrich meaning
  consolidate knowledge

- **transfer learnings and experiences to other contexts**

Key Points

The process of 'anchoring' is a way to solidify and transfer learning experiences.

'Anchoring' involves establishing an association between an external cue or stimulus and an internal experience or state.

Cues that are anchors can help to transfer learnings to other contexts.

Presenters may use anchors to reaccess states in themselves as well as in their audience.

Summary of Anchoring'
Reference Experiences (continued)

Types of 'Anchors'

• **Stimuli**

   voice tone
   gestures
   locations
   key words

• **Symbols**

   metaphors
   slogans

• **Universals**

   analogies
   common experiences

Key Points

The 'cue' used as an anchor may be either verbal, non-verbal or symbolic (the presenter may even become an anchor).

It is often useful for a presenter to preplan cues to be used as anchors.

Common objects and cues from the audience's working environment may make effective anchors.

Establishing and Anchoring Reference Experiences

In the same way that the richness of understanding with respect to a cognitive map could be assessed by how many of the senses are connected to it, the richness of a reference experience can be assessed by the degree to which it is connected to imagination, memory, or to ongoing experience.

Given a learning goal and a particular cognitive package, what sort of reference experiences might be created, given the type of audience, that would most accomplish the learning goal? In which kinds of cases is memory valuable, versus imagination or ongoing demonstrations? In addition to the representation of information, reference experiences are the essence of an effective presentation.

One issue has to do with the degree of transferability of a particular reference experience. A written scenario might stimulate a person to get access to remembered or constructed experience, but because it's not interactive, when that person returns to his or her interactive reality, the new learning is not connected.

Anchoring-Elaboration Cycle

Another issue has to do with the ability to establish anchors to help transfer learning experiences to other environments. An anchor is best established by first associating the cue with the experience, then going through a cycle in which the experience is continually elaborated and the anchor repeated. The 'elaboration - anchoring' cycle is a useful way to reinforce learnings and associations.

After the initial association is made, the presenter will want to 'elaborate' the number of connections by stimulating and anchoring associations such as, "How does this apply to your work?" "How does this relate to your family?" "How does this relate to a friend, or an ongoing situation?" This is not simply a repetitive reinforcement, it's an enrichment and an elaboration of the space of experience which one is trying to anchor to something.

The more that can be elaborated or elicited with respect to a particular concept or reference experience, the stronger that anchor will tend to be. For example, music often affects people because of what was happening when they first heard a particular song. Something important or something significant in their life was going on and the song happened to be on the radio. This is the essence of 'nostalgia'.

The more that a person is committed, the more will be learned, and the more will be anchored. If one is able to anchor something to a stimulus that already has associations crossing multiple contexts, and is not so specialized, than there is an automatic transfer factor built in.

Further, if one is able to widen the space of what one is presenting to show its relevance to other people, one has also elaborated what one is anchoring. If one is able to draw out other reference experiences, and then return to the same anchor, the richness of that anchor is elaborated. If there is a personal association such as a family experience, and there is an association to a classroom experience, and an imagined experience, then the anchor has a wider base of reference experiences.

Another issue is, how many contexts is it likely that a particular anchor can be taken in to? If the anchor is the presenter, unless he or she follows the learners around, the presenter has anchored the rich experience to himself or herself. When people leave the classroom, they might like the presenter and be very enthusiastic, but not be able to apply what they have learned.

One can anchor by returning to specific examples, stories, or jokes. Think about being with a group of friends. When you repeat a story about some experience, you recreate the same feeling that you had when you were together before.

The word 'anchoring' is itself an anchor. During this discussion we have been connecting a number of different reference experiences to the term 'anchor'. 'Anchoring' is the term we keep coming back to elaborating the richness of its meaning.

Exercise

The purpose of the next exercise is to explore how to create reference experiences that are most easily connected to the relevant cognitive package and generalized to the learner's reality.

The process will be similar to the exercise for creating cognitive maps. First form small groups. Each person will pick an idea or concept that is important for his or her audience to understand, remember and connect to their professional reality. Each person is then to determine what kinds of reference experiences (if any) are typically used to illustrate or demonstrate that idea or concept. Each person is then to come up with other kinds of reference experiences might be used to improve either the strength of the connection or the transfer of the capability to the reality of a particular audience. Keep in mind that creating reference experiences for 'why' will be different from creating reference experiences for 'how'. Particular cognitive packages might have different requirements in terms of the various experience levels, in terms of whether the emphasis is just on the 'what', or the 'why' and the 'what'. Explore what kinds of reference experiences might have to be attached to the kind of level of learning required by the cognitive package.

The group members are then to take turns leading the group through the reference experience and attempting to 'anchor' the experience. The presenter may use key words, voice tone, gestures, physical location, or some other form of 'anchor'.

Afterwards, the group will discuss what was different and effective about the new reference experiences and the 'anchor'.

Exercise 4: Creating and Anchoring Reference Experiences

Form a group of four. Each person will take a turn being the presenter.

1) Each group member picks an idea, skill or concept that is important or challenging for his or her audience to understand, remember or connect to their professional reality (the group may choose to all use the same topic).

2) Each group member individually determines what kinds of reference experiences (if any) are typically used to illustrate or demonstrate that idea, skill or concept. Think in terms of whether it is ongoing, remembered or constructed. Also consider which level of learning is important to emphasize - what, how, why, who.

3) Each group member individually comes up with another type of reference experience (ongoing, remembered or constructed) for the same idea, skill or concept that will make it more effective.

4) One at a time, each group member individually leads the group through the reference experience and attempts to 'anchor' the experience using key words, voice tone, gestures, physical location, or some other form of 'anchor'.

5) The group discusses the impact and effectiveness of the new reference experience and the anchor.

Following the discussion, the group rotates to the next presenter.

Summary of Establishing and Anchoring Reference Experiences

Issues Related to 'Anchoring'

When
- timing of 'stimulus'

What
- cognitive knowledge versus emotional or motivational states
- positive or negative experiences

How
- planned versus spontaneous
- reinforce versus elaborate

Why
- reaccess
- enrich
- transfer

Who
- self versus others

Key Points

An anchor is best established by first associating the cue with the experience, then going through a cycle in which the experience is continually elaborated and the anchor repeated.

The 'elaboration - anchoring' cycle is a useful way to reinforce learnings and associations.

Key Points (continued)

The transferability and duration of an anchor relates to:
1) How often it is reinforced
2) The intensity of the experience being anchored
3) The perception of the relevance of the anchor and how it can be applied

A successful experience may become anchored to different elements of the context which produced the success.

Internal experiences can become anchors for other internal experiences through the process of association.

part two

Strategies for Designing and Implementing Effective Presentations

Assessing the Audience

Basic Relational Skills

Non-Verbal Communication Skills

Assessing and Managing One's Internal State

Phases of Planning a Presentation

Overview of Part Two

Strategies for Designing and Implementing Effective Presentations

The purpose of Part Two is to:

1. Explore the behavioral and non-verbal aspects of making effective presentations.
2. Define ways to observe and model effective presentations skills in oneself and others.
3. Enrich readers' presentation abilities through the exploration of several techniques and strategies for interacting with an audience.
4. Define ways to transfer effective abilities across different contexts and to other people.

Part Two is made up five chapters:

Chapter 5   Assessing the Audience

Defines the observational skills necessary to recognize and 'calibrate' key states and responses in others.

Chapter 6   Basic Relational Skills

Describes basic interactive skills for understanding and establishing rapport with different types of audiences.

Chapter 7   Developing Non-Verbal Communication Skills

Defines the basic areas of non-verbal communication involved in making presentations and explores the skills necessary to non-verbally support one's presentation.

Chapter 8 Assessing and Managing One's Internal State

Provides a set of distinctions and a method for presenters to identify and reaccess internal states related to effective performance.

Chapter 9 - Phases of Planning a Presentation

Provides a method for planning and evaluating an effective presentation based upon the 'storyboarding' strategy of Walt Disney.

Assumptions

The material to be covered in Part two is based on a set of *assumptions* about the interaction between a presenter and the audience:

There is no one right way to learn or teach. There is a diversity of strategies which may produce more or less effective results depending on the characteristics of particular individuals, the learning task and the context.

Different people have different maps of the world, different motivations and learning styles. Developing the communication and relational skills necessary to manage this diversity is an important aspect of making effective presentations.

Different styles of learning and presenting are more effective for different learners, learning tasks and different phases of the learning cycle.

There is a difference between the form and content of one's strategies for learning and presenting. Certain process elements of a presentation that are effective in one context may or may not also be effective in other contexts.

People's abilities to learn and perform effectively are influenced by different levels of experience which have some elements that may only be perceived through the introspection of personal subjective experience, and others that may be tracked by the observation of external cues.

One's ability to present effectively is influenced by one's perceptions of a situation, one's internal state and the choices one perceives possible or available in that situation.

Subjective cognitive processes are accompanied by micro behavioral patterns which serve to support those cognitive processes and to provide external cues relating to those processes.

Effective presentation skills may be enhanced or transferred by the identification and manipulation of cognitive patterns and micro behavioral cues.

Chapter 5

Assessing the Audience

Defines and develops the observational skills necessary to recognize and 'calibrate' key states and responses in others.

- **Some Issues Related to Effective Presentations**

- **Applications of Observational Skills in Communication**

- **Micro Behavioral Cues**

- **Assessing an Audience**

Some Issues Related to Effective Presentations

People learn in different ways and different learning tasks require different approaches. The fact that people have different maps of the world is a factor that can either be a positive factor or, if mismanaged, a negative one in an organization.

One principle of communication is that certain kinds of presentation styles might be effective in certain kinds of contexts but be less effective in others. Another important principle of communication is that how one presents one's communication or information will greatly affect how it is perceived by the other person. And the more flexible one is in one's map and presentational style of behavior, the more effective a professional communicator one will be.

One conclusion that we might begin to draw from what we have covered so far is that different contexts, functions and roles might require different strategies to achieve effective performance. People who have certain kinds of thinking styles, or aptitudes, might find themselves more suited to certain kinds of contexts. Their way of thinking might naturally fit the strategies and skills required for a certain function. This is something positive, in that these differences allow people to effectively serve different functions. The challenge then becomes unifying these different ways of thinking, through some kind of a macro level strategy, which manages these differences towards some kind of common goal.

There are also macro level expressions of these different types of strategies, even in cultures. For example, in the past several decades there has been a big difference between American and Japanese approaches to the development of technology. American technology companies tend to be oriented toward big breakthroughs and visions of new and innovative technologies. The creative style of Japanese technology companies, on the other hand, has been to incrementally refine something to make it better and better. Both are effective, but in different ways.

The structure of the learning and teaching process is related to the T.O.T.E. Any structured activity is oriented around a goal and an ongoing feedback loop directing one toward the goal.

On a micro level we've said that the effectiveness and richness of the functioning of this feedback loop depends on certain fundamental processes relating to how information is represented and presented in the form of:

1) cognitive packages and

2) reference experiences

On a macro level, there are different kinds of learning and teaching styles that might be associated with processes related to:

a) the mix and balance of different elements of presenting (e.g. task versus relationship)

b) the degree of emphasis on different levels of experience (environment, behavior, mental capabilities, beliefs and values, identity)

c) the types of information channels and filters used in setting goals, defining evidences and selecting operations for making a presentation

Summary of Some Issues Related to Effective Presentations

Some Issues Relating to Effective Presentations

- **People think and learn in different ways.**

- **There are different types of communication and relational skills related to different types and stages of presentations.**

- **A key issue in making a presentation is how to manage different cognitive and relational processes in individuals and groups.**

Key Points

There are differences between individual learning strategies.

Different kinds of learning strategies are effective for different contexts and tasks.

Different micro strategies are indicative of different general thinking styles.

The effective management of organizational learning involves the coordination of different learning styles.

Applications of Observational Skills in Communication

An important skill in making presentations is the ability to observe behavioral cues associated with particular attitudes and responses. Attitudes are often expressed through micro behavioral cues. As you become aware of these kinds of cues, some of them can become quite obvious, especially in situations where people are acting spontaneously.

Physiology also provides a powerful leverage to recognize and influence other people's states and thinking processes. Physiological cues can become 'anchors' to manage one's own state and the states of others in order to reproduce or access positive experiences and effective performances. By having an awareness of physical cues, you have a tool to help people enter an effective state regardless of the context.

For instance, you may have observed during presentations that, at times, people tend to imitate the behaviors of another person. When people interact and begin to establish rapport with each other, oftentimes there's a kind of matching of certain behaviors that starts to happen. This process is called "pacing." If you begin to watch people, you will notice that when they really have rapport with each other, they do a lot of mirroring of each other's behaviors. This is a basic principle of communication that can be used as a tool to help manage people more effectively.

In fact, one way of insuring that you don't interfere with somebody's thinking or learning process when you are communicating with them is to assume elements of their behavior, to 'put yourself in their shoes'. Of course, it is easier to do this with people who know each other and already have rapport. It's almost like an acknowledgment of rapport in that case. But in situations involving people who you're not familiar with, it might be difficult and even appear disrespectful. One suggestion in that kind of situation would be to do it in stages such that you pace one element at a time. Perhaps voice tone first and then gestures, etc.

In this chapter we will explore how physiology can be used to help manage the states and learning processes of others by:

1) establishing rapport with people through the process of pacing and matching their general behavioral patterns

2) understanding or feeling people's world views more fully by mirroring key elements of their physiology,

3) drawing information about people's internal processes from their physical cues and helping to reaccess or add to states and cognitive patterns associated with effective performance

Summary of Applications of Observational Skills in Communication

Application of Observational Skills in Communication

1. Establishing 'rapport' with another person through 'pacing' ('mirroring')

2. 'Calibrating' another person's internal responses

3. 'Anchoring' and reaccessing positive experiences

Key Points

Physiology can be used to help manage the creative processes of others by:

1) establishing rapport with people through the process of pacing and matching their general behavioral patterns
2) understanding or feeling people's world views more fully by mirroring key elements of their physiology
3) drawing information about people's internal processes from their physical cues and helping to reaccess or add to states and cognitive patterns associated with learning

Micro Behavioral Cues

Words are only one of the ways that people communicate. A person's non-verbal communication is as important, if not more so, than his or her verbal communication. Words typically represent the things that a person is conscious of while most non-verbal behavior is out of awareness. People will offer you a large number of unconscious non-verbal cues that can be used if you train yourself to observe and respond to them.

One principle of communication is that human beings display how they are thinking in various subtle ways. It is possible for one to recognize signs of thought in another person and detect particular patterns. For instance, certain behavioral cues indicate how people are thinking—such as whether they are visualizing, hearing sounds or words, or feeling. Once the thought process is discovered, one can vary one's own communication techniques to match the other person's and, therefore, establish easy rapport.

Body posture is an important influence on one's state. For example, most people would probably find it very difficult to learn effectively with their heads down and their shoulders hunched forward. If you put yourself into that physiology, you will find it's going to be difficult to be inspired. When people are visualizing, for instance, they often tend to be in an erect posture. When people are listening, they tend to lean back a bit with their arms folded or heads tilted. When people are having feelings, they tend to lean forward and breathe more deeply. These cues won't necessarily tell you if the feeling is positive or negative; only that an individual is accessing feelings. So somebody might be feeling very relaxed and have the same general posture as somebody who's feeling depressed.

Voice tone can be a very powerful cue. When people are visualizing, they will tend to speak in a slightly higher and faster tone of voice. When people are into feelings, they're voices are often lower and slower in tempo. These types of vocal patterns can affect people's states. For example, if a presenter says in a low slow voice, "Now I want you to listen to this complex concept very carefully," you would probably feel more like going to sleep than observing. Similarly, if a presenter says, "Okay everybody, really get relaxed and comfortable!" in a very rapid and high pitched voice, you might experience a different kind of incongruity. Voice tone and tempo can serve as a cue to trigger cognitive processes. Attention to the sense of hearing is often triggered by melodic voice changes and fluctuations of tone, tempo and rhythm.

Gestures are another important behavioral cue. People often gesture to the sense organ that is most active for them in a moment. People will touch or point to their eyes when they are attempting to visualize something or when they get an insight. People gesture toward their ears when they are talking about something they heard or are trying to hear. Likewise, people will touch their mouths when they are thinking verbally (like Rodin's *The Thinker*). When people touch their chest or stomach, it generally indicates feeling.

Eye movement patterns are one of the most interesting micro behavioral cues. It has been said that "The eyes are the windows of the soul." The eyes are also considered a window to the mind. Where a person's eyes are looking can be an important cue. Eyes up tends to accompany visualization. Eyes to the left and right go along with listening. Eyes down accompany feeling. An eye position to the left is often indicative of memory, while a movement to the right indicates imagination.

People often give clues or cues about their thinking process through language. For example, somebody might say, "I just *feel* that something is wrong." This statement indicates a different sensory modality than somebody who says, "I'm getting a lot of *static* about this idea," or somebody who says, "It's very *clear* to me." Each statement indicates the cognitive involvement of a different sensory modality.

Of course, some cues are going to be idiosyncratic. They are unique to a certain person, like some of the cognitive aspects of a person's thinking style. There are other kinds of cues that are shared by many people. You might find, for example, that certain kinds of gestures might vary in their meaning from culture to culture but other kinds of physiology and physiological cues might also be shared from culture to culture like facial expressions.

The ability to recognize both idiosyncratic and cultural cues is an important skill for a presenter.

Summary of Micro Behavioral Cues

Types of Cues

Each individual has his/her cues for different states.	Some cues - e.g. gesture - change between cultures.

- 'Individual' (idiosyncratic) cues and 'common' cues of:

    - a group
    - a culture

    must be learnt in order to manage a presentation

Key Points

Physical activities influence neurological activities and vice versa.

Certain micro behavioral cues may be associated with cognitive processes.

These micro behavioral cues can be used to 1) identify certain aspects of unconscious mental processes and 2) mobilize or reactivate processes related to cognitive patterns or physiological states connected to effective performance.

Assessing the Audience

To present effectively one needs to be able to assess the audience. The two most important aspects of an audience relative to communication and relational issues involve 1) their attitude and 2) their internal state. These determine the way a presenter will most likely need to adjust the interactive aspects of his or her presentation to be most effective with that particular audience. Attitude relates to the audience's general reaction to the context and type of material. Internal state relates to the particular emotional and physical mood of the group. Attitudes are associated with beliefs and values and tend to remain more constant through time. Internal states are affected by a number of factors (such as time of day, previous events, etc.) and are more changeable.

A presenter's observational skills are necessary to determine the attitude and internal state of an audience and individual audience members.

It is important to have the skill to observe without interpreting when managing others. While making a presentation it can be difficult to appreciate the differences in the micro physiology of people's states unless you are very accurate in your observation because most of their behaviors are often quite subtle. This kind of accuracy involves a certain commitment of observation which you may not feel you always have time for. On the other hand, there might be certain contexts where it's worth the investment of precision - for example, with a key person in the audience or in a moment where it becomes very important in terms of what's happening in your interactions. A top manager once made the comment that, "There are moments where a leader has to have the ability to change the second half of his sentence based on the feedback he received to the first half of the sentence." Not that you would always do that, but sometimes circumstances require that commitment of observational skill.

"CALIBRATION" is the name given to the process of learning how to read another person's responses in an ongoing interaction. Instead of prejudging or hallucinating about the internal responses of their audiences, good presenters learn to read responses in the ongoing situation. For example, let's say that a presenter had noticed that every time a learner talked about feeling "confused" she furrowed her eyebrows, tightened her shoulder muscles and clenched her teeth slightly. If at some time later he observed these same cues as the learner was listening to a certain part of a presentation, he would have evidence that she is experiencing the "confused" response and may respond appropriately to it.

Having the sensory awareness to make these kinds of observations is a critically important skill in all parts of communication. One way to sharpen your skills in this area is to practice reading another individual. For example, ask a friend or associate to think of something he or she was really satisfied with. As they are thinking of it observe their facial expression, eye movements and postural changes. Then ask them to think of something that they were dissatisfied with and carefully observe again. You should be able to see some differences in their non-verbal response to the two thoughts. Finally, ask them to think of one or the other of the two experiences but not to tell you which one it is. Then "read their mind" by seeing which set of cues you observe as they are thinking, and telling them which thought it is. You may be surprised at how accurate you can be.

Exercise 5: 'Calibration' Developing Observational Skills

"Calibration" involves linking behavioral cues to internal cognitive and emotional responses. Find a partner and try the following exercise.

1. Ask your partner to think of some concept that your partner feels he or she knows and understands.

2. Observe your partner's physiology closely. Watch your partner's eye movements, facial expressions, hand movements, etc.

3. Then ask your partner to think of something that is confusing and unclear. Once again, watch your partner's eyes and features carefully.

4. Notice what is different between the patterns of features.

5. Now ask your partner to pick either concept and think of it again.

6. Observe your partner's features. You should see traces of one of the clusters of features associated with either understanding or confusion.

7. Make a guess and then check with your partner to find out if you were correct.

8. Have your partner think of other concepts that he or she understands or finds confusing and see if you can guess which category they fall into. Confirm your guess by checking with your partner.

9. Then explain some concept to your partner and determine whether your partner has understood it or is unclear or confused by observing his or her features. See if you can determine the moment the understanding occurs.

Summary of Assessing the Audience

Assessing the Audience

Key Characteristics of an Audience

- Internal State

- Attitude

Observational Skills For "Calibrating" the State of Individuals and a Group

Key Points

Because a person's internal states, cognitive processes and attitudes are expressed through micro and macro physical cues, the pacing or mirroring of physical cues helps to gain an understanding or feeling of another person's world view.

Chapter 6

Basic Relational Skills

Assists participants to develop basic interactive skills for understanding and establishing rapport with different types of audiences.

- **Establishing Rapport with a Group**

- **Basic Perceptual Positions in Communication and Relationships**

- **Establishing Rapport with a Group by Building Second Position**

Establishing Rapport With a Group

One of the most important relational skills of a presenter is the ability to establish RAPPORT with his or her audience. The quality of information you can communicate to a group will directly relate to the amount of rapport you have with them. People generally experience more rapport with people who share the same model of the world they do.

Matching language patterns is one way of going to someone else's model of the world. Identifying and incorporating key words, micro metaphors and examples commonly used by an audience or audience members is a way of sharing their maps of the world and attaining rapport.

Pacing or subtly mirroring their non-verbal communication can also greatly enhance their experience of rapport because they will perceive you as being "like them". Some ways to non-verbally pace or mirror a person include putting yourself into a similar body posture, using similar intonation patterns and expressions, dressing similarly, etc. This is a powerful form of putting oneself 'into the shoes' of another person

To be an effective presenter is critical to keep in mind that EVERYBODY HAS HIS OR HER OWN MENTAL MAP OF THE WORLD. When a person wants to communicate something or understand something, that person will construct a mental map of the idea or concept. It is the job of the presenter to recognize (and in some instances to help develop) the thinking styles of their audience and to provide as many options and choices as they can that will fit those styles.

As an analogy, consider for a moment which of the following houses would appeal to you the most:

The first house is quiet and picturesque. It has a very quaint look to it. You can see that a lot of focus has been put on the colorful patio and garden area. It has a lot of window space so

that you can enjoy the view. It is clearly a good buy.

The second house is very soundly constructed and situated. It is in such a quiet area that all you hear when you walk outside are the sounds of the birds singing. Its storybook interior tells of so much character that you'll probably find yourself asking yourself how you could ever pass it by.

The third house is not only solidly constructed, it has a real special feel to it as well. It's not often that you come in contact with a place that touches on so many important features. It is spacious enough that you really feel like you can move around freely and yet cozy enough that you won't wear yourself out taking care of it.

Which one did you choose?

Actually, these are all descriptions of the same house! The only difference is that each description was written to appeal to a different sense. If you chose the first house you are probably more visually (sight) oriented. If you chose house number two you are most likely more auditorally (sound) oriented. If you chose the third, you probably value your feelings more than your other senses.

People's maps of the world are constructed from experiences they perceive through their sensory representational systems. People will often find themselves more at home with one sense than the others as they build their mental maps. For some people "seeing is believing;" others rely much more heavily on their feelings; while others value what they hear and seek the verbal opinions of other people.

The visual learners say, "People learn best by seeing demonstrations. People learn by watching. Can you do more demonstrations?" Kinesthetic learners, on the other hand, say, "I get confused by demonstrations. People learn by doing. Can we do more exercises?" And, of course the auditory learners say, "People learn best by listening and discussing. I can always practice on my own. Could you talk some more about your thoughts and experiences?" People have different strategies. Therefore, it's always good to do a bit of talking, a bit of demonstrating, and a few exercises in order to appeal to everybody.

In general, if you are communicating something to a group of people you want to take a multi-sensory approach. If you are making a presentation you might ask yourself, "How do I demonstrate this visually? How do I demonstrate it so the people get a feel for it? How do I demonstrate this so they hear it?" People learn in different ways and it is important to cover all the different styles.

One of the key abilities of an effective presenter is to recognize and respect other people's models of the world. If you can do this, you can benefit from diversity-otherwise you will constantly fight it.

Pacing and Leading

Once it is discovered how people are thinking—by watching for non verbal cues and/or listening for language patterns—one can adapt one's own language and behavior to harmonize with them and establish rapport. This is accomplished through the process of 'pacing and leading'

Pacing is the process of using and feeding back key verbal and non verbal cues of the other person, in order to match his model of the world. It involves having the flexibility to pick up and incorporated other people's vocabulary and behavior into one's own vocabulary and actions. The process is important to all of the essential aspects of effective communication, (such as rapport and trust building. When you are pacing, you are trying to step into another person's shoes and experience their model of the world. In pacing you want to communicate with someone in their own language and through their own existing way of thinking.

Leading involves the attempt to get another person to change, add to or enrich his or her behavior or thinking process by subtly shifting one's own verbal and behavioral patterns in the desired direction. The basic idea of pacing and leading is to incrementally introduce somebody to changes in their behavior or world view by first matching and acknowledging and then widening their model of the world. For instance, when people are learning or being introduced to something new, it is best to start with something familiar and then move to something new.

Most people think of presenting as being primarily associated with leading. But often the most effective presenters are those who can first enter into another's world view and meet them at their own model of the world.

A good example of the power of pacing and leading comes from a sales seminar for a telemarketing group. There was one customer that no one had been able to sell. It turned out this person talked very s...l...o...w...l...y... But he was the president of a big company that could become a real key customer. People would call him and say, "Hello, sir, I know you're a very busy man, if I could just take a minute of your time," speaking at about twice his speed.

But that isn't the way that person thinks, or listens. As a way to improve communication skills, a member of the group was instructed to call this man up and say, "Hello... (very slow)... I'm from xxx company... and I'd really like to have some time... to talk with you.... when you really have some time... to think about our products... I know it's really important for you... to take your time and think about things... Could you tell me when we could call...." and so on. Instead of saying, "I'll only take a minute." You say, "When could I call you back when you would have enough time to think about this comfortably and thoroughly?" The company president felt so comfortable with the approach that he scheduled a meeting, and the telemarketing group ended up getting the account.

One of the most important outcomes of pacing is the establishment of rapport. When people know you can think as they do and can take their world view into account, they are much less resistant to new ideas.

There are a lot of ways of pacing someone. In addition to matching voice tone and tempo, you can match key words such as representational system language and physical posture. One way to pace someone at a very deep level is to speak at the rate which the other person is breathing. You speak in tempo with their breathing rate.

This can even help to deal with problem people at a presentation. For example, during a presentation on communication skills, a man stood up and said, "You say all this stuff! It's too easy. I'm in the REAL WORLD. This stuff is for seminars. I just don't feel that it will work with MY clients." So the presenter said, "Why don't you come up and be a demonstration subject. You pretend that you're one of your difficult clients in the real world, and we'll try to get a hold of how this might put you more in touch with them."

So he came up and started "role playing." The first thing the presenter did was to subtly put himself into a similar body posture. He said, "Well, I'm a busy man. I have to see a hundred people like you every day. Most of them are full of crap and end up wasting my time. Let's hurry up and get through this." As the presenter responded to him he began to match his speech to the man's breathing, and said, "It sounds to me... like you want someone... you feel you can trust... Someone who cares.... about what you need... Think of somebody you have really trusted... in your life... and how you felt... That's the kind of relationship... I'd like to develop with you." The presenter continued pacing his breathing, and finally after about three minutes of this the man stopped him and said, "You know, I was going to try to be as resistant as I could, but right now I'd buy anything from you."

Some Exercises to Practice Pacing and Leading Skills

One of the most effective ways to develop the skill of pacing and leading is to practice it with another person while being observed. The following exercises each emphasize different skills of pacing and leading. Each exercise involves the same set of roles:

A=Learner
B=Presenter
C=Observer

It is usually preferable if person A is not aware of the specific task of person B, as it might make B overly self conscious.

After each exercise the observer should make comments on what he or she noticed about the behavior of person A (learner) *in response to* the behavior of person B (the presenter). Person A is to report on his or her thoughts, feelings and sense of rapport with person B.

Non-Verbal Rapport

The first exercise explores the relationship between verbal and non-verbal matching. B first matches A both verbally and non-verbally. Then B mismatches A verbally while matching non-verbally. After that B matches A verbally while mismatching non verbally. Finally B returns to matching A both verbally and non-verbally. The effects on person A are likely to be different depending upon the representational channel the A attends to the most. If A is verbally oriented he may be more effected by the verbal mismatching. If A is more visually or physically oriented he may be quite sensitive to B's non-verbal matching or mismatching.

1. B enters into a conversation with A, asking for A's opinions about various subjects.

2. While B is conversing he or she is to begin to subtly match aspects of A's physiology (including voice tone and tempo). This is most easily done in the context of continual 'backtracking' or 'active listening'.

3. When B is fully "mirroring" A, B can check the degree of rapport by leading - that is, B changes some minute element of B's own physiology and notices if A follows.

4. When be is convinced that there is sufficient rapport established, B is to verbally disagree with one of A's opinions but continue to match physiology. (C is to calibrate whether A is in rapport or having difficulty relating to B).

5. B is then to physically mismatch A, but verbally agree with one of A's opinions. (C is to calibrate whether A is in rapport or having difficulty relating to B).

6. B concludes by once again physically matching A and calibrating for rapport.

Pacing and Leading During Calibration

Pacing and leading can be used to influence the direction of a person's thoughts. In this exercise, Person B attempts to direct A to make a particular association by pacing the physiology exhibited by A while thinking of particular experiences.

1. B is to ask A to think of someone A really finds 'exciting and interesting' and someone A finds 'boring' and to calibrate the differences in A's physiology.

2. B is then to continue questioning A about the two people while mirroring the physiology A assumes while talking about them. This is most easily done by B continually 'backtracking' each of A's comments (i.e., 'active listening').

3. B is then to lead A into thinking of one or the other the people during the guessing part of the exercise by leading A into the physiology she or he associates with that person while asking, "Randomly choose one or the other of two and think of that person now."

Crossover Mirroring

A presenter cannot always directly mirror the behavior patterns of others. In this exercise Person B practices pacing and leading by coordinating a pattern of his or own behavior with a different pattern of behavior in person B.

1. B enters into a conversation with A. B is to find something that is ongoing and repetitive in A's behavior (such as breathing rate).

2. B is to 'mirror' or pace the repetitive behavior with some other behavioral pattern - i.e. B paces A's breathing by nodding his or her head in rhythm with A's breathing rate. (This is most easily done in the context of 'back-tracking' or 'active listening'.)

3. B tests 'rapport' by incrementally shifting the "cross-over" behavior and noticing if A's repetitive behavior shifts in a corresponding manner.

Summary of Establishing Rapport With a Group

Pacing and Leading

'Pacing' = Matching or mirroring another's pattern of behavior
- Matching or using key words
- Mirroring gestures
- Speaking in a similar tone of voice

'Leading' = Incrementally changing one's own behavior in order to direct or shift another's pattern of behavior to something else
- Inserting or adding new words
- Incorporating new gestures
- Shifting voice tone or tempo

Key Points

'Pacing' (matching, mirroring) another's verbal and non-verbal cues helps create rapport.

Once 'paced', individuals or groups can be 'lead' to different states or thinking processes by shifting relevant verbal expressions or physical cues.

Basic Perceptual Positions in Communication and Relationships

Our perceptions of ideas or experiences are greatly affected by the point of view or perspective from which we consider them. There are three basic "perceptual positions" from which a communication situation may be viewed. Perceptual positions refer to the fundamental points of view one can take concerning the relationship between oneself and another person:

> *1st Position:* Associated in your own point of view, beliefs and assumptions, seeing the external world through your own eyes.

> *2nd Position:* Associated in another person's point of view, beliefs and assumptions, seeing the external world through his or her eyes.

> *3rd Position:* Associated in a point of view outside of the relationship between yourself and the other person.

Probably one of the most important relational skills a presenter can develop is the ability to switch points of view and take multiple perspectives of a situation or experience. Try taking the different perceptual positions with respect to a presentation situation by practicing the following steps.

1. Think about a challenging presentation you have made or are planning to make.

2. Put yourself fully into 1st position by imagining that the audience is here right now and that you are looking at them through your own eyes.

3. Now imagine you are "in their shoes" looking at your self from their eyes. Assume the perspective, beliefs and assumptions of the audience as if you were one of them for a moment.

4. Now view the relationship between yourself and the audience as if you were an observer watching a video of a presenter interacting with an audience.

Notice how taking the different perceptual positions changes your perception of the experience. What new awareness did you get about yourself, the audience or the situation?

Summary of Basic Perceptual Positions in Communication and Relationships

Basic Perceptual Positions in Communication and Relationships

- **'First Position'**
  Through one's own eyes and world view

- **'Second Position'**
  In the 'shoes' of the other

- **'Third Position'**
  From the perspective of an observer

Key Points

There are 3 basic fundamental Perceptual Positions to be taken with respect to every communication and relational context.

1st person point of view - self.

2nd person point of view - others involved in the situation.

3rd person point of view - an uninvolved observer.

Putting oneself into the shoes of the audience is an important skill for making an effective presentation.

Taking '2nd position' with another allows one to clarify the extent of one's knowledge about the world view of the other and find the areas where more clarity is needed.

Establishing Rapport with a Group by Building Second Position

Assessing an audience involves gathering information about learners and their needs. It requires determining not only what people need, but also how they learn. It also involves understanding their values, their beliefs, and their perceptions of themselves.

In the next exercise you will practice putting yourself into somebody's else's shoes and exploring their point of view in relationship to yourself.

Form a group of four. Each person is to identify some topic or concept and a typical or challenging audience. The group members are to role play the audience by putting themselves into the shoes of the audience. Audience members are to take the point of view of the intended receivers and evaluate how well they understand the topic, and more importantly, how much rapport they experience with the presenter.

Before making the presentation, the presenter is to take second position with the audience by stepping into their perspective. From this second position perspective, the presenter should think of what kinds of words, examples, metaphors, voice tone, etc. would help to get rapport with the audience. In other words, what would an audience member like most to see and hear from a presenter?

To deepen the second position perspective, the presenter can consider 1) what cognitive capabilities are required to understand the topic. What does it presuppose that the audience needs to know how to do? 2) Are there issues of motivation or belief that the topic presupposes? How does the topic fit with the audiences values and motivations? 3) How does the audience perceive itself? Some people might have limiting self-concepts in relationship to certain kinds of information. They might think "This is isn't relevant", or

"I'm not mathematical", or "This is too complicated". What are their self perceptions.

The value of doing this kind of second position exercise before making a presentation is that either you a) clarify your understanding of the audience perspective or b) realize you don't know the answer and need to gather more information. It tells you what aspects of your audience you already know and what aspects you need to find out more about. You may not know what sort of values it would require from the learner. If you can't answer one of those questions, it identifies areas of research and further assessment.

Taking second position with an audience ahead of time also provides a way to help you adapt your presentation in the moment. It is important to always keep in mind that, even if you go out and do a needs assessment, "the map is not the territory." You may have done extensive research, and yet when you walk into the classroom or presentation situation, you find a different group than you were expecting. For that reason you will want to continually be entering the shoes of the audience at key points during the unfolding of the program itself. It is valuable to be continually checking out the audience perspective.

The presenter is to incorporate the information gathered from second position into his her presentation to the audience, applying the skill of 'pacing and leading' to achieve and maintain rapport with the audience during the presentation.

After the presentation the group and the presenter are to compare their perceptions of the audience and discuss what was effective about the presentation, especially with respect to the degree of rapport experienced by the audience. The presenter is to reveal which cues or thinking styles he or she was attempting to pace and lead.

Exercise 6: Establishing Rapport With a Group by Building Second Position

1. Presenter defines a topic and a typical or challenging audience

2. Group members are to role play the audience

3. Presenter goes to 'second position' with the audience and thinks of what words, examples, metaphors, voice tone, etc. would help get rapport with the audience.

   The presenter may deepen the second by considering three levels of analysis:

   a) The skills or capabilities presupposed. Does the topic presuppose that one already know something else or how to do something else. What kind of conscious or unconscious competence is assumed.

   b) The values and beliefs presupposed. The topic might be dealing with beliefs about the company, as well as individual values. What is the belief system of this audience? What does the audience believe about the presentation and the presenter?

   c) The audience's perceptions of themselves. What kinds of identity issues, or role identity issues, might either be addressed or presupposed by the topic?

4. Presenter presents the topic and attempts to achieve and maintain rapport using the information obtained from 'second position'.

5. Group discusses what was effective and impactful in terms of the sense of rapport and the presenters ability to successfully 'pace and lead'.

Chapter 7

Developing Non-Verbal Communication Skills

Defines the basic areas of non-verbal communication involved in making presentations and explores the skills necessary to non-verbally support one's presentation.

- **Messages and Meta Messages**

- **Basic Non-Verbal Communications Skill for Making Effective Presentations**

- **Uses of Micro Behavioral Cues**

Messages and Meta Messages

The effectiveness of people's ability to learn in a group is dependent on their ability to communicate with one another. Communication between the individual members of a group happens both verbally and non-verbally, and there are both verbal and non-verbal influences on the behavior of the group as a whole.

There are ways in which a presenter can non-verbally recognize and encourage positive states that come up spontaneously in a group. One method is called "shaping." Shaping has to do with encouraging something in a physiological way. For example, there is a story about a psychology professor who conducted an experiment with a group of university students. He instructed the students in his class to compliment or express approval for women who wore red sweaters. They were not to comment on the sweater itself but just say something like, "Oh, you look nice today," or to smile at them. Supposedly, after a week he walked into the dining hall and it was filled with women in red sweaters.

Apparently the students also decided to try the process on the professor himself. If the professor went to one side of the room when he was teaching, the students all agreed among each other to yawn and act bored. If he went to the other side of the room, they all sat up, nodded their heads and acted very interested. After a while the professor found himself doing all of his teaching from one side of the room!

Managers often do similar things, but generally they are unaware of what they are doing. For example, a top manager at IBM unconsciously used this process of shaping to direct people to 'discover' that they agreed with his approach. When he was talking with somebody who was thinking along similar lines as he was, he was a wonderful and very active listener, constantly making eye contact, nodding his head and saying things like, "Oh really?" "That's interesting." "Tell me more about your idea." If somebody started to go off in a direction he didn't like, he would stare blankly and mumble "Uh huh...Uh huh." It was like talking to a brick wall. As soon as the other person began to shift directions, the manager would come back to life and become very interested in the other person's direction of thinking. People found themselves eventually coming around to his way of thinking without understanding why.

These types of cues are considered 'meta messages'. The basic process of communication involves the transmission of both messages, which carry the content of a communication, and 'meta-messages', which are higher level messages about the content. Meta messages are messages *about* other messages. Meta messages are typically about a) the type or level of message being sent, b) a person's state or c) about the status or relationship between group members. People also send meta messages about the messages that they have received, like the IBM manager.

Meta messages are essential for the interpretation of a message. There is a difference between what a person 'says' and what he or she 'means' or intends. The message received is not always the message that was intended or sent. And in practical reality, the meaning of a communication to another person is what that person received regardless of what was intended.

The framework of managing the interplay between messages and meta messages involves 3 fundamental ongoing micro communication processes:

1) Using observational skill and feedback to reduce distortions between intended and received message,

2) Determining the selection and combination of messages and meta message,

3) Ensuring that the micro messages support the larger message and lead in the direction of the communication outcome.

Summary of Messages and Meta Messages

The Influence of Verbal and Non-verbal Communication

There are two types of messages in communication:

1. Verbal content
2. Non-verbal meta messages:
   Messages about the kind of verbal message being sent

Meta messages are necessary in order to interpret the message.

- Metamessages are often analogical, e.g.:
  - Voice tone
  - Emphasis on one part of a sentence
  - The intensity of facial expressions
- Within a group meta-messages are often 'about' relationships.

Key Points

Effective communication involves both messages and 'meta messages'. 'Meta messages' are messages about other messages which help the receiver interpret the full meaning of the message.

Meta messages are typically the non-verbal part of the communication.

Meta messages commonly relate to the context, state, relationship or level of focus in which the message is being sent or is to be received.

Basic Non-Verbal Communication Skills for Making Effective Presentations

There are several classes of activities related to managing the relationship between messages and metamessages in the presentation context:

1) Selecting and chunking the whole message into the content elements and metamessages.

2) Determining by what channels message and metamessage elements will be sent.

3) Recognizing and responding to received messages and metamessages as feedback.

An effective communication strategy involves elements which are preplanned and aspects which are selected or adopted in response to feedback. The preplanned aspects of determining metamessages for a presentation essentially relate to how information is prepared and delivered. For example, having the same message in a manual and on a transparency is a meta message about the significance of the information. The degree of engineering of material or simply the amount of it is a meta message about how much time has been spent on it. Whether printed material is given at the beginning of class or handed out during the progression of class is a meta message about how to perceive that information with respect to the other information that has been presented.

The face-to-face aspects of managing messages and meta messages are primarily related to the non-verbal behavior and responses of the presenter and the audience. In face-to-face communication, meta messages are most often transmitted non-verbally. People are constantly sending meta messages, even when they themselves are not talking. Linguists call this the 'grunts and groans' phenomenon. When people are listening they are often making noises like "Ah," "Uh huh," "Hhmmm," etc. As it turns out, these noises are not just random. If somebody is rapidly going "Ah ha, ah ha, ah ha," it indicates he or she is receiving the message differently than if that person slowly says, "Ahhh haaaa."

The same message will have different meanings if accompanied by different non-verbal metamessages. For example, consider the difference in the implications of the following messages:

"You should not be doing *that* here."

"You *should not* be doing that here."

"*You* should not be doing that here."

Based on the placement of voice inflection, the message takes on different implications relating to a particular level of emphasis: You (identity) should not (beliefs/values) be doing (capability) that (behavior) here (environment). It is the presence or lack of such meta messages that often determines how a message is interpreted and whether a message will be interpreted appropriately. For example, if a presenter says "YOU weren't respecting the rules," this is much more likely to be taken as an identity message. If the presenter says, "You weren't respecting the RULES," then he or she is not emphasizing the individual identity so much as the level of why and how.

A typical non-verbal skill is the ability to use voice stress. If a presenter says, "Now I want you to pay attention to what I will say next," in a monotone voice it will probably not accomplish the intended purpose of getting the audience's attention. The same message with a different voice, stress as a metamessage that would give it a different meaning. The presenter could say, "I want you to *pay attention* (with voice emphasis) to what I'm going to say next." That non-verbal aspect of the communication will have an influence on how people receive that message. Learners are often given so much information that a key question for them is what to emphasize, what's important? This is typically done through the non-verbal metamessages that accompany the information.

Somebody even experimented with the influence of meta messages in relation to the computer. One of the problems with a computer is that it doesn't give meta messages. So, he decided to program the computer to give meta messages to the people who were using it. The computer would constantly print responses like, "Oh yes." "I see." "Very good." It turned out that people really liked using this computer! They were actually more productive with the computer because they somehow felt more rapport with the computer, even though they couldn't tell you why.

Different kinds of meta messages are used in different ways in different cultures. For example, someone once did a study on the interactions between people in English pubs and in French bistros. He found that the French touched each other on the average about 110 times per hour. The English touched each other only an average of three times per hour.

Metamessage are not only voice stress; they come from other non-verbal aspects of presenting. In addition to voice inflection, some other ways in which a presenter sends non-verbal metamessages are through gestures and the movement of his or her body. Setting up the presentation room in a certain way is a metamessage about the kind of interaction that you want people to have.

The geographical relationship between group members is an important non-verbal influence on group process. It often has both a physical and symbolic influence on shaping the interaction between group members. For example, sitting in a circle, as in a round table, encourages certain kinds of feedback and interactions between group members than sitting at a rectangular table or in a 'theater style' arrangement. A round table also conveys a different kind of symbolic relationship between group members. This influence is called 'psychogeography'.

Shaping Exercise

One simple non-verbal communication skill is that of shaping. It relates to the type of reinforcing influence that a person's non-verbal behavior has on the actions of another person (like the IBM manager described earlier). The following is a simple exercise on shaping involving three people: A, B and C.

1. B enters into a conversation with A. B 'shapes' A by subtly 'reinforcing' some aspect of A's behavior with a non-verbal 'meta-message' (e.g., facial expression, voice tone, etc.).

2. C tries to detect which of A's behaviors is being shaped and what reinforcing cue B is using.

Summary of Basic Non-Verbal Communication Skills for Making Effective Presentations

Basic Non-Verbal Communication Skills for Presentations

Ability to use meta messages
- Voice Tone
- Gestures
- 'Spatial Anchors'

Ability to recognize meta messages

Ability to respond to meta messages as feedback

Key Points

There are several classes of activities related to managing messages:

1) Selecting and chunking the whole message into the content elements and metamessages.

2) Determining by what channels message and metamessage elements will be sent.

3) Recognizing and responding to received messages as feedback.

Uses of Micro Behavioral Cues

One of the key influences on how effective a presentation is relates to the state of the group. The state of a person, influences that person's ability to learn and his or her degree of motivation. State has to do with the internal experience of the learners. Are they tired? Are they angry? Are they skeptical?

A person will receive a message differently based upon his or her state and the perceived status of the presenter. If the presenter is considered an expert, people perceive a message differently than if they consider the presenter to be a peer. If people are very excited, they will perceive messages differently than if they are distracted. As an analogy, as a metaphor, think about the body as being a kind of circuitry. If one changes the circuitry, one can put in the same information and get a different result. The kinds of states most relevant to a presentation include: attention, motivation and concentration.

What kinds of influences are there on a person's state that one can address as a presenter? What affects people's states? Some key influences on the state of a group are, 1) the environment, 2) their physiology, 3) the presenter's metamessages.

The environment is certainly a significant influence on people's states. The temperature, the lights, the setup of the room are stimuli that affect a person's physiology.

Another big influence on people's states is their own physiology. If a person sits in a certain way long enough, it's going to affect that person's breathing and other micro behaviors that influence cognitive processes. If you sit up straight and breath fully in the chest, it's going to be hard to fall asleep. So a presenter can do things to shift physiology.

A third important influence is the non-verbal metamessages of the presenter. One key use of meta messages relates to identifying and influencing one's own internal states and the state of an audience. Non-verbal micro behavioral cues can provide a powerful leverage to change other people's states and thinking processes. The presenter could say in a very flat monotone, "Now I'm going to talk to you about something very important for the seminar so that...". Or the presenter could say, "NOW! I'm going to talk to you about something VERY important!"

Physiological cues are also 'anchors' to manage one's own state in order to reproduce or access a particular state at will. By having an awareness of our own physical cues, you have a tool to help you enter an effective state regardless of the context. It is also possible to non-verbally anchor processes in a group by associating certain cues with the state of a group. For example, when a group is in a particularly productive state of learning, a presenter can give some kind of stimulus like clapping his or her hands or giving an encouraging gesture. Pretty soon, if he or she claps or makes the encouraging gesture, it begins to be like a trigger for the effective state.

Thus, the presenter should be able to recognize and respond to not only the learning style of audience members, but also the internal state of himself and the learners. At least the presenter needs to be able to factor that into his or her communication strategy. Some of the basic uses of micro behavioral cues and metamessages are to:

1) Reaccess positive states in oneself and others.

2) Manage one's own state to achieve optimal performance.

3) Influence and direct the ongoing states of others.

Different types of meta messages may be more or less effective for influencing states depending on the other influences on the state. A presenter may be able to do something to change the state of a group, or he may not if the influence that produces that state is so much outside of the immediate moment. If a group of people has just been told that they're going to be fired, this is going to affect their state in such a way that the presenter may need to just accept that state and status as an operating constraint. At other times, a group's state can be changed by simply taking a coffee break.

Exercise 7: Non-Verbal Communication in Presentation

Managing one's own state and the state of the audience is one of the most important and influential skills of a presenter. Non-verbal cues are often one of the most relevant and influential aspects of managing internal states. In this exercise we will explore some of the uses of non-verbal communication in making an effective presentation.

1. Presenter picks a topic that is important or challenging to present.

2. Presenter defines a set of meta messages he or she would like to communicate in relation to that topic including:

   • his or her own state
   • type of relationship he or she wants to have with the audience
   • the desired state for the audience to be in
   • level of focus of the communication

3. Presenter determines how he or she could use voice tone, gestures, spatial location, etc. to communicate the meta message.

4. Presenter makes a short presentation incorporating the intended meta messages.

5. After the presentation, each group member records the meta message he has 'received' by answering the following questions:

   • What state was the presenter in?

- What type of relationship did the presenter want to have with you (the audience)?

- What kind of state did the presenter want the audience to be in?

- What was the level of focus emphasized by the presenter? (where, when, what, how, why, who)

6. Group and presenter compare 'intended' and 'received' meta messages.

Summary of Uses of Micro Behavioral Cues

Uses of Micro Behavioral Cues

- **Reaccess positive states**

- **Manage one's own states**

- **Influence the states of others**

Key Points

One key use of meta messages relates to identifying and influencing the internal states of an audience.

The kinds of states most relevant to a presentation include: attention, motivation and concentration.

Physiological cues are 'anchors' to manage one's own state in order to reproduce or access a particular state at will.

Behavioral cues can be 'paced' or matched in order to establish rapport with someone.

Chapter 8

Assessing and Managing One's Internal State

Provides a set of distinctions and a method for presenters to identify and reaccess internal states related to effective performance.

- **Effective Performance and Personal States**

- **'Circle of Excellence': Micro Behavioral Analysis**

Effective Performance and Personal States

The states of both sender and receiver influence the flow of the communication. States act as both a filter and bias in receiving and interpreting messages. How do we purposefully trigger or operationalize effective performance? How does someone go about getting access to cognitive and behavioral process in a consistent way?

In this chapter we are going to explore some tools to enhance personal performance and to capture or focus moments of effective performance. These same tools can also be used to re-access an effective state if you've been distracted or interrupted.

A good deal of what happens during an effective performance is unconscious. Many key aspects often happen outside of conscious awareness. In addition to instruments and tools that allow us to bring unconscious thoughts into awareness, it is also useful to have some ways of encouraging and actually directing or utilizing unconscious processes as well.

States are often influenced by metamessages and are themselves a metamessage about what sort of information is being sent or received. A core skill for an effective performance is to recognize the connection between behavioral cues and patterns to internal cognitive structures and unconscious processes. In addition to the mental strategies and observational skills related to the process of presenting, there are also physiological and behavioral aspects. Certainly, there are language cues that might be used to stimulate, trigger or encourage a person's performance. There are also purely behavioral cues.

For example, the founder of a large shipping company claimed that he used physical activities to help him solve problems. For certain problems he would have to go out and play golf to get in the frame of mind required to deal with the issues. For other problems, he would go out and ride his bicycle in order to think about it effectively. He was so specific about which type of physiology to use that he would say, "You can't golf on that problem. That's one that you have to ride your bicycle on."

The point is that physiological activities stimulate and organize other neurological activities. Riding a bicycle is a macro level activity. There are also micro physiological and behavioral cues and processes that accompany cognitive processes.

Effective teaching and learning is a function of a person's state as well as his or her mental processes. It is important to acknowledge the influence of behavior, even very subtle aspects of physiology, on performance. If you observe athletes getting ready to perform, they clearly prepare their state through certain kinds of physical cues. Similarly, presentation ability is influenced by a person's state which can be adjusted through certain kinds of macro and micro level behavioral cues.

Sometimes performance is state-dependent, too state-dependent. This is illustrated in the American movie "Butch Cassidy and the Sundance Kid." The Sundance Kid was a gunfighter who was a great shot, but he could only shoot if he was moving. If he tried to stand still, he couldn't hit anything, he had to be jumping or falling or twisting in order to aim. This is an advantage but also a limitation. Similarly, some people can only be effective when they're under stress.

Different people have different motivations for teaching and learning. Some people are effective when they are going towards something. Others are more effective when they are trying to avoid something. There is a saying that, "When the going gets tough, the tough get going." The implication is that a difficult situation forces strong people to draw more fully on their inner resources. The problem arises for these kinds of people when there is no difficult situation. They have to create one in order to get going. Physiological cues give us tools to influence our state as well as the cognitive processes associated with effective teaching and learning.

There are macro cues like body posture and gestures, and there are more subtle micro or minimal cues.

In this chapter we will investigate the relationship between physiology and performance. The exploration of the influence of physical state on the learning and teaching process is important to both complete and balance our understanding of the learning process.

Contrastive Analysis

One of the simplest and most profound ways of finding relevant behavioral cues is through what is called "contrastive analysis". In this case, this would involve contrasting states of effective performance with states of being stuck or distracted.

For example, think of a time you made an inspired presentation and put yourself back into that experience as fully as possible. Then contrast that state with a time that you wanted to be inspirational but were either distracted or interrupted. Notice which behavioral cues, both obvious and subtle, change between the two states.

Even very subtle behaviors can make a difference in performance. If you can find some of these cues, you can help to reaccess that state in a more conscious and purposeful way.

Of course, some cues are going to be idiosyncratic. They are unique to a certain person, like some of the cognitive aspects of a person's creativity strategy. There are other kinds of cues that are shared by many people. You might find, for example, that certain kinds of gestures might vary in their meaning from culture to culture but other kinds of physiology and physiological cues might also be shared from culture to culture like facial expressions.

In terms of your own personal performance, what's important is developing as much meta cognition or awareness of your idiosyncratic cues as you can. This can provide you with a way to tell if you are in a state conducive to making an effective presentation and offers a tool to get back into an effective state when you need to. The more you know about both the cognitive and physiological aspects associated with your own peak performances, the more chance you have of being able to re-access it at will.

In terms of managing the processes of others, many people have a tendency to assume that others are effective in the same way they are and that behavioral cues mean the same thing for everybody. This can create problems, especially with people who you work with. Developing an awareness of shared and idiosyncratic cues can help avoid problems of interpretation of the behavior of others.

Summary of Effective Performance and Personal States

The contrastive analysis of positive or limiting experiences uncovers the differences.

How a person thinks in an experience in terms of
Sensory representations:
• Images
• Internal language
• Emotions

How physiology is and changes in terms of
• Body posture
• Breath
• Voice
• Gestures

Key Points

Some states are more effective for presenting than others.

Effective states may be modelled and enriched.

Contrasting different states is a powerful way of identifying which kinds of physical cues and cognitive patterns are most relevant.

Relevant behavioral cues and cognitive patterns for personal excellence can be discovered by contrasting effective states to stuck states or problem states.

'Circle of Excellence': Micro-Behavioral Analysis

The goals of the exercise we are going to do next are to 1) discover something about your own cues for an effective state and 2) learn to observe and read other people's cues more effectively. You might discover something that you haven't been aware of related to the physiology associated with personal states that affect your ability to present effectively. You will also begin to develop an awareness about the kinds of cues that might be valuable in terms of recognizing and managing the states of other people.

This exercise is to be done in a group of three. One person will be the "explorer." The explorer is the person who's reliving the different experiences of effective versus stuck states. Person two will be an observer of the explorer's physiology. Person three will be a guide who will be giving the explorer directions and corroborating the observations of the observer.

Using the charts provided in the book, the guide will direct the explorer to think of a time when he or she was able to present effectively. The explorer is to relive this example of personal excellence as fully as possible. Both the observer and the guide will observe for significant behavioral cues using the guidelines provided in the book. The guide will then ask the explorer to think of an experience in which he or she was stuck or distracted. Observer and guide are to compare the behavioral cues for the two states.

Observer and guide should then make comments to the explorer on what they have observed. It is important for this exercise to remember the difference between observing and interpreting. Saying, "You looked comfortable," is not an observation, it's an interpretation. The skill here is to actually describe the behavior you observed, such as, "Your head was up"; "Your hand was on your face"; "You were leaning forward;" etc. Otherwise you're going to get into disagreements based on personal interpretations.

To test your observational skills, the guide can then ask the explorer to pick a different situation in which he or she was either effective or stuck but not to verbally reveal which one it was. The guide and observer will try to guess whether it was an example of the effective state or not. Once they have guessed, the explorer can validate or correct the guess.

Keep in mind that the purpose of this test is not to try to hide the answer but to learn to read each other better.

When you are done with this first part of the exercise, take another few minutes and discuss with each other which kinds of macro behavior you typically use to prepare yourself for a presentation. Do you ride a bicycle like a shipping company executive? Some people sit quietly and go through a mental dress rehearsal. Others get up and walk around a bit. Share some of the different ways you stimulate effective performance through macro behaviors in addition to micro behaviors.

Body Posture and Performance

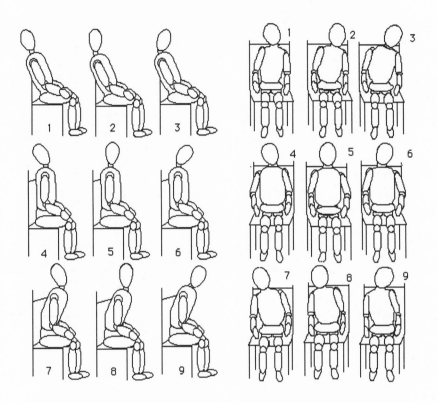

Circle the pictures that most represent your posture when you are presenting effectively. Put a square around the pictures that most represent your posture when you are stuck or distracted (choose both a front and a side view).

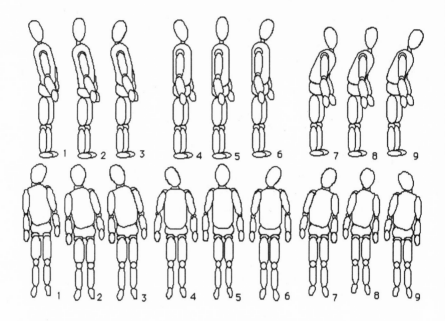

Circle the pictures that most represent your posture when you are presenting effectively. Put a square around the pictures that most represent your posture when you are stuck or distracted (choose both a front and a side view).

Gestures and Effective Performance

Circle the picture that most represents the gestures you most often use in making an effective performance, or draw the gestures on the picture provided on the right.

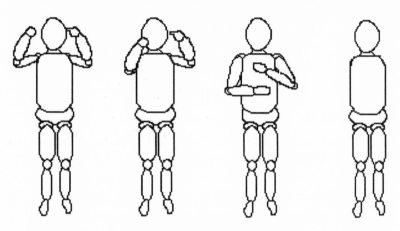

Effective Performance

Circle the picture that most represents the gestures you most often use in a stuck or distracted state, or draw the gestures on the picture provided on the right.

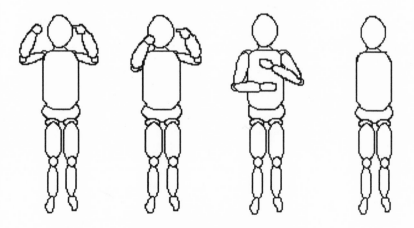

Stuck or Distracted State

Summary of 'Circle of Excellence': Micro-Behavioral Analysis

Exercise: 'Circle of Excellence' Micro-Behavioral Analysis

1. Contrast an experience in which you were able to present effectively with one in which you experienced difficulty.

2. Compare patterns of physical cues and what happens 'inside' the mind.
   - What is different?

3. Imagine a 'circle of excellence' on the ground in front of you. Locationally 'anchor' your effective presentation state by stepping into the circle only when you are fully in the effective state.

Key Points

"Calibration" involves the connection between observable behavior and internal subjective experience.

Key Points (continued)

Having an awareness of the micro and macro behaviors associated with your internal states is a valuable tool for increasing presentation ability.

Being able to observe the micro behavioral cues of others provides insight into their thinking styles and is an important tool in facilitating and managing the learning process of others.

Chapter 9

Phases of Planning a Presentation

Provides a method for planning and evaluating an effective presentation based upon the 'storyboarding' strategy of Walt Disney.

- **Phases of Planning**

- **Physiology and the Creative Cycle**

- **Well-Formedness Conditions for Evaluating a Plan**

- **Planning a Presentation**

Phases of Planning

Walt Disney's ability to connect his innovative creativity with successful business strategy and popular appeal allowed him to establish an empire in the field of entertainment that has survived decades after his death. Disney embodies the ability to make a successful company based on constant improvement and innovation. He represents the process of turning visions into concrete and tangible expressions through organization and planning. In a way, Disney's chosen medium of expression, the animated film, characterizes the fundamental process of all creative genius: the ability to take something that exists in the imagination only and forge it into a physical existence that directly influences the experience of others in a positive way.

One of the major elements of Disney's unique genius was his ability to explore something from a number of different **perceptual positions**. An important insight into this key part of Disney's strategy comes from the comment made by one of his animators that,*"...there were actually three different Walts: the **dreamer**, the **realist**, and the **spoiler**. You never knew which one was coming into your meeting."*

This is not only an insight into Disney but also into the process of creativity and effective planning. Any effective plan involves the coordination of these three subprocesses: dreamer, realist and critic. A dreamer without a realist cannot turn ideas into tangible expressions. A critic and a dreamer without a realist just become stuck in a perpetual conflict. A dreamer and a realist might create things, but they might not be very good ideas without a critic. The critic helps to evaluate and refine the products of creativity. There is a humorous example of a boss who prided himself on his innovative thinking abilities but lacked some of the Realist and Critic perspective. The people who worked in the company used to say, "He has an idea a minute...and some of them are good."

The point is that effective planning involves the synthesis of different processes or phases. The Dreamer is necessary to form new ideas and goals. The realist is necessary as a means to transform ideas into concrete expressions. The critic is necessary as a filter and as a stimulus for refinement.

Certainly, each one of these phases represents a whole thinking strategy all on its own - strategies that more often tend to conflict with each other rather than support each other. Of course, the specifics of how Disney used and coordinated his imagination ("the dreamer"), methodically translated those fantasies into a tangible form ("the realist") and applied his critical judgment ("the spoiler"), are something that we need to explore in more depth.

Overview of Disney's Strategy

Perhaps the most comprehensive description of how Disney's 'Dreamer', 'Realist' and 'Critic' operated in conjunction with each other comes from Disney's statement that:

*"The story man must **see clearly** in his own mind how every piece of business in a story will be put. He should **feel** every expression, every reaction. He should get **far enough away** from his story to take a **second look** at it...to **see** whether there is any dead phase...to **see** whether the personalities are going to be interesting and appealing to the audience. He should also try to **see** that the things that his characters are doing are of an interesting nature."*

The first part of the description focuses on the interaction between the dreamer and the realist. It is clear that the "second look" is the domain of the 'spoiler'.

Certainly, the statement defines three distinct perspectives.

1) The 'Dreamer' - Vision, whole movie:
"The story man must see clearly in his own mind how every piece of business in a story will be put."

2) The 'Realist' - feeling and action, first position, associated, moving:
"He should feel every expression, every reaction."

3) The 'Spoiler' - second position, distant:
"He should get far enough away from his story to take a second look at it.

a) Whole movie
"to see whether there is any dead phase."

b) Individual character, disassociated, still:
"to see whether the personalities are going to be interesting and appealing to the audience."

c) Individual character, disassociated, moving:
"He should also try to see the things that his characters are doing are of an interesting nature."

Disney's "second look" provides what is called a *'double description'* of the event. This 'double description' gives us important information that may be left out of any one perspective. Just as the differences in point of view between our two eyes gives us a double description of the world around us that allows us to perceive depth, Disney's double description of his own creations served to give them an added element of depth.

Of particular interest is that the "second look" involves a specific reference to being 'far enough away'. If it was too close, it could be overly influenced by the other perceptual positions. Similarly, it could also overly influence them. If the spoiler is too close to the dreamer, it may inhibit those dreams.

Summary of Phases of Planning

Creative Cycle for Planning Presentations

Dreamer
- Visionary
- Sees Big Picture
- Believes Anything is Possible

Realist
- Action Oriented
- Short Term Steps
- Acts "As If" a Goal is Possible

Critic
- Logical
- Avoids Problems by Finding What is Missing
- Asks "What If" Problems Occur?

Key Points

Planning a presentation is a process that involves the coordination of three sub-processes or phases. These phases may be generally designated as 1) Dreamer, 2) Realist and 3) Critic.

The Dreamer focuses on the 'big picture' with the attitude that anything is possible.

Key Points (continued)

Disney's process of 'realizing' his dreams took place through his physical association into the characters of the dream and through the 'storyboarding' process of chunking the dream into pieces.

The Realist acts "as if" the dream is possible and focuses on the formulation of a series of successive approximations of actions required to actually reach the dream.

Disney's process of critical evaluation involved the separating of himself from the project and taking a more distant 'second look' from the point of view of his audience or customers.

The Critic seeks to avoid problems and ensure quality by logically applying different levels of criteria (and checking how the product matches those criteria under various "what if" scenarios.)

Physiology and the Creative Cycle

As with other cognitive processes, physiology is an important influence on creativity and the ability to plan effectively. There are micro and macro level behavioral cues that accompany the Dreamer, Realist and Critic states that can help to more effectively enter the 'state of mind' necessary to plan an effective presentation.

For instance, think of what it is like when you are 'dreaming' or in the early stages of planning a presentation when there are many options and choices. What kinds of behavioral cues do you think are the most significant for your 'dreaming' process? What is your posture like? Do you move around? How do you orient your head and eyes?

Think of what it is like when you are 'realizing' an idea or 'dream' for a presentation . What kinds of behavioral cues do you think are the most significant for your 'realizing' process?

Think of what it is like when you are thinking 'critically' and evaluating your plan for a presentation. What kinds of behavioral cues do you think are the most significant for your 'critical' thinking process?

Which of the three types of thinking styles - Dreamer, Realist or Critic - seems to be the most natural for you?

Based on certain descriptions of Disney's behavior and the modeling of a number of different people who are effective in reaching these states, the following generalizations have been drawn about key patterns of physiology associated with each of the thinking styles making up Disney's creative cycle:

Dreamer: Head and eyes up. Posture symmetrical and relaxed.

Realist: Head and eyes straight ahead or slightly forward. Posture symmetrical and slightly forward.

Critic: Eyes down. Head down and tilted. Posture angular.

Summary of Section Physiology and the Creative Cycle

Physiology and the Creative Cycle

Physiology for 'Dreamer' State
- Head and Eyes Up
- Posture Symmetrical and Relaxed

Physiology for 'Realist' State
- Head and Eyes Straight Ahead or Slightly Forward
- Posture Symmetrical and Centered

Physiology for 'Critic' State
- Eyes Down Head Down and Tilted
- Posture Angular

Key Points

There are micro and macro level behavioral cues that accompany the Dreamer, Realist and Critic states.

Well-Formedness Conditions for Evaluating a Plan

The criteria used for the test phase of each of the stages of planning roughly correspond to what are called "Well-Formedness Conditions". These conditions are used to identify the minimum set of requirements a plan has to satisfy in order to be "well-formed."

Dreamer

1. Outcome is stated in positive terms; that is, it states what you do want as opposed to what you don't want.

Questions: *What do you want? What is possible? What is the payoff?*

Realist

2. Can be initiated and maintained by the person or group desiring it.

Question: *What specifically will **you** do to achieve this goal?*

3. Testable in sensory experience.

Questions: *How, specifically, will you know when you achieve the goal? What are the performance criteria? How will they be tested?*

Critic

4. Preserves the positive by-products of the current behavior or activity.

Questions: *What positive things, in any way, do you get out of your present way of doing things? How will you maintain those things in your new goal?*

5. Is appropriately contextualized and ecologically sound.

Questions: *Under what conditions would you not want to implement this new goal? Who and what else could it affect?*

What makes something well-formed is different at different stages. The criteria of the dreamer T.O.T.E. are primarily organized around possibility and desirability. The criteria of the realist T.O.T.E. are organized around feasibility and workability. The criteria of the critic T.O.T.E. are organized around acceptability and 'fit' in relation to the larger system.

Summary of Well-Formedness Conditions for Evaluating a Plan

Well-formedness Conditions for Evaluating a Plan

Dreamer
"WANT TO" Phase
- State the specific goal in positive terms.
- Establish the payoffs of the plan.

Realist
"HOW TO" Phase
- Ensure progress is testable through sensory experience.
- Establish time frames and milestones for progress.
- Make sure it can be initiated and maintained by the appropriate person or group.

Critic
"CHANCE TO" Phase
- Define the contexts in which   it is workable and problematic.
- Make sure it is ecologically sound and preserves any positive by-products of the current way(s) of achieving the goal.

Key Points

There are certain well-formedness conditions for defining outcomes and plans that offer useful guidelines for planning an effective presentation.

Different well-formedness conditions are more associated with different phases in the creative cycle.

Well-formedness conditions may be assessed on different levels (i.e., who, why, how, what, where, when).

Exercise 9: Planning a Presentation

Form a group of three: explorer, coach and observer.

1. For each phase of the planning cycle (Dreamer, Realist and Critic), the coach is to ask the questions relevant for that phase (listed below) and help the explorer keep track of his or her answers.

2. While answering the questions, the explorer is to assume and maintain the appropriate physiology and thinking style defined in the guidelines below.

3. Observer is to watch and ensure that the explorer maintains the appropriate state and does not 'contaminate' it.

4. Keep cycling through the phases to make successive approximations of the plan.

"WANT TO" PHASE - Dreamer

Objectives: (State the specific goal in positive terms; establish the payoffs of the idea.)

*"**What** do you want to do? "* (As opposed to what you want to <u>stop</u> doing, <u>avoid</u> or <u>quit</u>.)
"**Why** do you want to do it?" "**What** is the purpose?"
"**What** are the payoffs?" "**How** will you know that you have them?" "**When** can you expect to get them?"
"**Where** do you want the idea to get you in the future?"
"**Who** do you want to be or be like in relation to the idea?"

Level of Focus: What.
Cognitive Style: Vision - Define the 'big picture'.
Attitude: Anything is possible.
Basic Micro Strategy: Synthesizing and combining the senses.
Physiology: Head and eyes up. Posture symmetrical and relaxed.

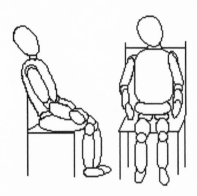

Dreamer State Physiology

"HOW TO" PHASE - Realist

Objectives: Establish time frames and milestones for progress; make sure it can be initiated and maintained by the appropriate person or group and that progress is testable through sensory experience.

"**How** specifically will the idea be implemented? **How** will you know if the goal is achieved?   **How** will the performance criteria be tested?"

"*Who will do it?*" (Assign responsibility and secure commitment from the people who will be carrying out the plan.)

"**When** will each phase be implemented?   **When** will the overall goal be completed?"

"Where will each phase be carried out?"

"Why is each step necessary?"

Level of Focus: How.
Cognitive Style: Action - Define the short term steps.
Attitude: Act 'as if' the dream is achievable.
Basic Micro Strategy: Associating into characters and 'storyboarding'.
Physiology: Head and eyes straight ahead or slightly forward. Posture symmetrical and slightly forward.

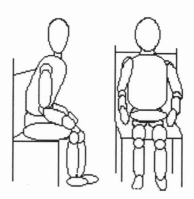

Realist State Physiology

"CHANCE TO" PHASE - Critic

Objectives: Make sure it is ecologically sound and pre-serves any positive by-products of the current way(s) of achieving the goal.

"Why might someone object to this new idea?"

"Who will this new idea affect and who will make or break the effectiveness of the idea and what are their needs and payoffs?"

"When and **where** would you <u>not</u> want to implement this new idea?"

"What positive things do you get out of our current way(s) of doing things?"

"How can you keep those things when you implement the new idea?"

Level of Focus: Why.
Cognitive Style: Logic - Avoid problems by finding what is missing.
Attitude: Consider 'what if' problems occur.
Basic Micro Strategy: Taking 'audience' perspective.
Physiology: Eyes down. Head down and tilted. Posture angular.

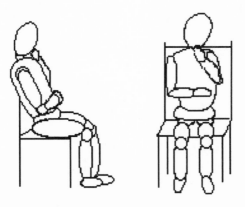

Critic State Physiology

Personal Application of Disney's Planning Strategy

We can also adapt the information about Disney's creative thinking strategies into a set of steps that may be used by an individual to prepare for a presentation.

1. Select three physical locations and label them (1) **'Dreamer'**, (2) **'Realist'** and (3) **'Critic'**.

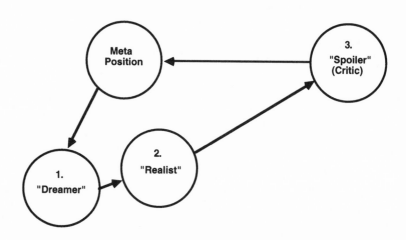

2.   Anchor the appropriate strategy and state to each physical location. Make sure the physiological state associated with each state stays 'pure.'

    a. Think of a time when you were able to creatively dream up or fantasize new ideas without any inhibitions; step into location (1) and relive that experience.

    b. Identify a time when you were able to think very realistically and devise a specific plan to put an idea effectively into action; step into position (2) and relive that experience.

c. Think of a time when you were able to constructively criticize a plan - that is, to offer positive and constructive criticism as well as to find problems. Make sure the location is far enough away from the others that it doesn't interfere. Step into location (3) and relive that experience.

3. Pick a presentation you are currently planning and step into the dreamer location. Visualize yourself making the presentation as if you were a character in a movie. Allow yourself to think about it in a free and uninhibited manner.

4. Step into the realist location, associate into the "dream" and feel yourself in the positions of all of the relevant characters. Then, see the process as if it were a 'storyboard' (a sequence of images).

5. Step into the critic position and find out if anything is missing or needed. Then, turn the criticisms into questions for the dreamer.

a. Remember, the critic is to criticize the plan, not the realist or the dreamer.

b. It is often helpful to have the critic initially acknowledge which elements of the plan are satisfactory before asking questions.

6. Step back into the dreamer position to creatively come up with solutions, alternatives and additions to address the questions posed by the critic. If the critic's questions seem too harsh or it is difficult to think of the questions without accessing the critic state, go to an Observer Position before returning to the dreamer location. You may even wish to rephrase the critic's questions from the Observer Position.

7. After you have repeated this cycle several times, consciously think of something else that you really enjoy and are good at but continue to walk through the dreamer, realist and critic locations. This will promote lateral thinking and unconscious gestation.

8. Continue to cycle through **steps 4, 5 and 6** until your plan congruently fits each position.

Summary of Planning a Presentation

'Installation' of Disney Strategy

- **Recall good examples of Dreamer, Realist, and Critic States and 'anchor' them to the different physical locations.**

- **Think of a presentation you are planning and bring it through the cycle of Dreamer, Realist and Critic by moving to the appropriate locations.**

Key Points

The locational sorting of the different processes helps to organize and coordinate them and avoid interferences or 'contamination' between the states.

Turning a criticism into a question helps to avoid the 'negative' effects of the critic and stimulate the Dreamer.

Once a creative cycle is robustly 'installed', it can be enriched by processes which stimulate lateral thinking and unconscious gestation.

part three

Managing the Interpersonal Aspects of a Presentation

Managing Interactions with a Group

Managing Resistances or Interferences

Conclusion: Principles of Effective Presentations

Overview of Part Three

Managing the Interpersonal Aspects of a Presentation

The purpose of Part Three is to:

1. Define the basic communication and relational skills required to manage different levels of learning and thinking styles within a group discussion or interaction.
2. Learn how to manage and enrich individual thinking styles.
3. Learn how to interact more effectively with a group.
4. Identify and develop skills necessary to manage the interactions of others in situations involving potential resistances or interferences.

Part Three is made up of three chapters:

Chapter 10 - Managing Interactions with the Group

Provides a set of distinctions and tools to recognize and direct different learning and thinking styles during a group interaction or discussion.

Chapter 11 - Managing Resistances or Interferences

Identifies and explores the communication and relational skills necessary to handle resistances and interferences within a group.

Chapter 12- Principles of Effective Presentations

Summarizes the key skills and issues explained in the book and establishes some of the basic operational principles of effective communication.

Assumptions

The material to be covered in Part III is based on a set of *assumptions* about the dynamic process of groups:

Groups, teams and organizations are natural systems and follow certain self-organizing principles.

The key element in an effective presentation is the awareness and management of different thinking styles and the different aspects of the learning cycle.

There are a number of different levels of processes which influence the learning process of a group.

There are different mixes of communication and relational skills that are required for different types of presentation contexts and situations.

The key to stimulating and managing the learning process in a group or team is in managing the process of communication between group members.

There are a number of different levels of messages sent and received during the communication between people, both verbally and non-verbally.

Managing a discussion or an interaction in a group is most effectively done through an incremental process of *pacing* and *leading*, and/or *acknowledging* and *adding to* the contributions of team members.

The core criteria for effectively managing a discussion or interaction in a group are 1) *thoroughness* of coverage of the perceptual space, 2) *relevance* of the issues addressed by the group given the perceptual space, and 3) *balance* of contribution of people in different roles and with different thinking styles.

People are essentially positively intended. Responding effectively to resistances and interferences within a group involves finding and acknowledging the intention or communication behind the resistance and offering other choices and alternatives to accomplishing that intention.

Chapter 10

Managing Interactions with the Group

Provides a set of distinctions and tools to recognize and direct different learning and thinking styles during a group interaction or discussion.

- **Managing a Group**

- **Types of Group Process and Experience Levels**

- **Basic Attitudes and Filters of Experience - Meta Program Patterns**

- **Identifying Basic Thinking Styles**

- **Skills Related to Managing a Group**

- **Backtracking' and Active Listening**

- **Process Oriented Language Skills**

- **Pacing and Leading During a Group Discussion**

Managing a Group

Effective group process is organized around the T.O.T.E. The operations of a group during a presentation or discussion are directed toward the goals that define the purpose of that presentation. The performance of the group is evaluated with respect to evidence indicating its progress toward its goal. To function effectively, it is important that group members share goals and evidence procedures. In order to accomplish common goals, however, a group's T.O.T.E. needs a range and diversity of operations and operators in the same way that an individual needs flexibility.

Different kinds of capabilities and thinking styles among group members are necessary to fulfill the various functions and roles required to reach goals. In an effective group, there is an awareness of the value of different capabilities and thinking styles. Managing a group involves the ability to identify and coordinate the different thinking styles of group members in order to most effectively achieve the group's goals.

In the processes of evolving, encouraging and drawing out the cognitive processes of group members, it is important to be able to identify and adapt to both physical and psychological constraints. Managing the learning cycle of a group involves establishing physical and psychological constraints which direct the group's process in relation to the phase of the learning cycle they are in. This accounts for many of the differences and variances between the T.O.T.E.s of different presenters.

The learning cycle in a group involves the movement from unconscious incompetence to conscious incompetence to conscious competence to unconscious competence. The development of conscious competence involves the movement between large chunks (the big picture of 'vision') and small chunks (the establishment of micro objectives to reach the larger goal). A key part of managing a group's learning process involves the ability to break down general concepts and actions into the specific cognitive and interactive processes required to implement or fulfill them.

For effective group learning, it is important to acknowledge and incorporate a) all of the thinking styles within the group (such as Dreamer, Realist, Critic, etc.) and b) to incorporate the different points of view of the group members in all three stages. One of the problems that can often arise during a discussion is that a person with the Dreamer style says something that is perceived as outrageous to which a Critic responds negatively. In reaction to the Critic, the Dreamer polarizes and starts defending the dream even more. The Critic complains and they go around and around in a vicious circle. Finally the Realist says, "We are running out of time. Let's get down to work." But it ends up as a chaotic mix of polarities. The cycle doesn't progress because the Dreamer is constantly being interrupted by the critic and so on.

Different thinking styles are likely to be more prevalent at different stages of the learning cycle:

Dreamer - unconscious incompetence
Realist - conscious competence
Critic - conscious incompetence

In an effective group, each would support or complement each other's strengths by having the dreamer output a number of ideas to a realist who outputs an approximation or plan to the critic, who evaluates the plan, etc.

An important criterion for managing in a group is to maintain balance. On the one hand, a presenter needs to draw out as full a range of potential as possible in group members. On the other hand, it is also important to draw out and utilize individual strengths.

Some people have strengths as a Dreamer or Realist or Critic. One way to stimulate participation is to try to develop the flexibility of everybody to cover different perceptual spaces. Another strategy is to identify and then utilize the particular strengths of certain individuals, but avoid categorizing them in a way that 'pigeon holes' them.

Managing the relationship and rapport between group members is a crucial element in the kind of communication strategy a presenter uses to guide the process of a group. In fact, in some cases, the effort of managing a group might be 80% in terms of relationship and 20% in terms of task. Stimulating participation and effective performance in groups often involves working more with the relationships between people than the context that they are working with. Consider some of the highly effective learning environments you've been in yourself. How important were the relationships with people in addition to the context that you were learning?

Relationships create the space for learning. Some kinds of learning tasks are best accomplished with the learner by himself. Others are best achieved through small groups discussing or comparing performances. Still others are most effectively facilitated by information shared in a whole group. The influence of relationship is different depending on the type of learning task in which the group is engaged.

Managing the Mix of Task and Relationship

There are a number of contexts in which teaching and learning are required and enacted in organizations. These contexts involve varying mixes of relationship and task elements and of varying orientations toward solving problems or achieving goals.

A basic issue involved in making an effective presentation involves determining the appropriate mix of problem versus outcome orientation of a presentation, and the relative emphasis of a particular learning task on the behavioral or task aspects versus the relational aspects.

Determining the specific context of a particular presentation involves defining the learning task to be accomplished, the relationship between the presenter and the audience and the relationship between the members of the audience. Different audiences may have a diversity of roles, motivations and attitudes in relation to one another and the material to be presented. Thus, different learning contexts, audiences and tasks might require different approaches and presentations styles.

A 'coaching' strategy, for example, involves a lot of emphasis on both task and relationship. The role of a mentor often involves primarily supporting the learner as an individual, focusing on his or her learning process more than on a specific task. 'Presenting', on the other hand, requires more of an emphasis on content or task than relationship. Because of the nature of the typical presentation context, the degree of personal relationship is less essential than for a coach or trainer. A learning situation emphasizing relationship over task would be that of 'mentoring'.

It is important to separate the skills and processes of presentation from the content of the presentation. The same communication and relational skills may be applied in different contexts; but a particular presentation style that is effective in one context may not be as effective for others. An effective presenter needs to have the skill and flexibility to

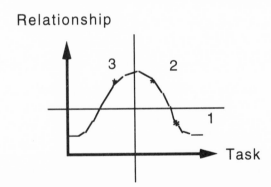

1. Presenting: High Task - Low Relationship.
2. Coaching: High Task - High Relationship.
3. 'Mentoring': Low Task - High Relationship.

recognize different learning contexts and adapt his or her presentation style accordingly.

Summary of Managing a Group

Managing a Group

1. Goals, evidence, and operations are different in each stage of the learning cycle: unconscious incompetence, conscious incompetence, conscious competence, unconscious competence.

2. The various stages of the learning cycle must be balanced.

- The conscious competence stage should not be favored at the expense of the other stages.

- It is important to appreciate all stages and learning styles and identify positive intentions and effects.

- Different learning styles correspond to each stage.

Key Points

Balance is a core criterion in managing the dynamics of group learning. No one thinking style should be favored at the expense of the others.

The effective management of group learning in a group involves the continual recapitulation and incorporation of the different perspectives of all group members.

Different thinking styles are more likely to be prevalent at different stages of the learning cycle.

Summary of Managing a Group
(continued)

Managing the relationship is crucial for effective presentations

- In learning contexts, communication is often 80% related to the relationship and 20% to the task.

- Managing a group effectively means working on the relationship in order to 'create space' for effective learning processes.

- The influence of the relationship is different depending on the type of context.

Key Points

Managing the relationship and rapport between group members is a crucial element in the effective learning process of a group.

The influence of relationship is different depending on the type of learning context.

Types of Group Process and Experience Levels

In forming a communication strategy, it is important to remember that there are different types of group goals related to different levels of group process (who, why, how, what, where and when). The different levels of *what, how* and *why* are a particularly significant aspect of group process. In managing others, it is important to consider the values, beliefs and the kinds of 'T.O.T.E.s' that the group is operating from. Often, the situations that people perceive as limiting or constraining are due to their assumptions or beliefs concerning the contexts they consider to be appropriate or permissible to participate in. For instance, the beliefs and values shared by group members will affect their sense of motivation and permission. If group members are lead to perceive mistakes as failures instead of feedback, the group might be more stressed.

There are different verbal cues associated with different levels of experience:

- Identity is associated with language like: "I am a ..." or "He is a ..." or "You are a ..."

- Belief level language is often in the form of statements of judgments, rules and cause effect, e.g. "if ... then ..." "one should ..." "we have to ..."

- The level of capabilities is indicated by words such as "know", "how", "I am able", "think", etc.

- Behavioral level language refers to specific behaviors and observable actions, e.g., 'do', 'act', 'walk', 'say', etc.

- Language at the environmental level refers to specific observable features or details in one's external context, e.g., white paper, high walls, large room, etc.

There are different levels of operations to stimulate and manage the learning process of a group. Some operations could be on the level of environment and behavior - establishing the *where*, the *when* and the *what* in terms of time frames, constraints and actions. Other operations involve establishing plans, thinking styles and meta programs to promote effective learning and draw out individual competencies - the *how*. Clearly, operations on the level of the *why* - beliefs and values - are particularly significant for group process. There are also operations on the level of the *who*. Creating a team spirit involves the establishment of the identity of the group. Thus, there are different types of strategies that may be used by a presenter for addressing issues of 'want to', 'how to', 'chance to' and 'who to.'

A complete communication involves defining all of the relevant levels associated with the task: who, why, how, what, where, when. An effective presentation will address all of the levels necessary to achieve the learning goal. Thus, an important added aspect of the presenter's communication strategy for working with the group is the coordination of different levels of process. This is where the different levels of process become important.

When managing a discussion, for example, a presenter might not define goals in terms of specific objectives, but rather in terms of values or the desired effect to be manifested by the group. It might be important to initially maintain flexibility with respect to the *what*, but consensus with respect to the *why*. A communication strategy might encourage consensus about *who* and *why*, but differences and diversities of perspectives with respect to *how* and *what* . If there are too many different opinions relating to *why* and *who*, the differences are more likely to produce conflict rather than being productive.

Generally, the most effective groups will have shared goals and shared evidences, but will acknowledge and encourage individual differences with respect to capabilities and actions. A particular presentation may require more emphasis on one level than on the others. The purpose of some presentations is to communicate how to do something. Others are more related to inspiring people and establishing values. Others are focused on clarifying roles with a system.

Thus, managing a group involves the alignment of different levels of experience, i.e., actions, plans, beliefs, values and roles. Thus, managing a group is a multi-level process. In an effective group, the 'what' is connected to the 'how', 'why' and 'who'; that is, the behavior of the group takes place within the context of a plan, a set of values and a sense of role identity or 'group spirit'. A behavior that is not connected to values is just an empty 'technique'. This is an especially important issue with respect to effective teaching and learning.

People sometimes make the mistake of focusing on the behavioral aspect of a process that somebody has applied successfully. But when that behavior becomes separated from the inspiration, values and beliefs that were all part of the system that made the process work to begin with, then people are just 'going through the motions'. The techniques become trivial or simply rote reactions. Assuming a particular physiology, for example, is just an act if you are not also accessing the *how* and the *why* of that behavior.

The process of learning can be likened to cooking. A teacher is like a chef. Typical lessons tend to focus on the *what* and are like a particular recipe. Communication strategies require addressing the *how* and the *why* and are more like learning how to cook.

A lot of learning naturally arises from the interaction between different levels of process. A group is influenced by both micro and macro level processes. Cognitive strategies and behavioral patterns will influence individual group members on a micro level. But groups are also guided by more general process - such as the 'outcome frame'.

A group often has dynamics that transcend the specific styles and proclivities of the people who make it up. For example, regardless of any particular individual physiology, certain general cognitive patterns are related to different phases of the learning cycle. An important part of managing a group on a macro level relates to the general attitude of the group and its members. One important challenge in managing the process of a group is how to maintain structure and a common attitude among all group members without interrupting or discounting their individual abilities.

We have explored some ways to identify and calibrate the micro processes of individuals. There are also distinctions related to the more general patterns of people's interactions and attitudes in a group. These patterns are called 'meta programs'. 'Meta program' patterns are general classes of attitudes that are associated with how people sort information on a macro level.

Summary of Types of Group Process and Experience Levels

Types of Group Processes and Experience Levels

- 'Creating a group spirit' is at the 'Who' level.

- 'Establishing common values and assumptions' is at the 'Why' Level.

- 'Identifying and managing different learning styles' is at the 'How' level.

- 'Defining specific behaviors and operations' is at the 'What' level.

- 'Defining the timing of operations and packages' is at the 'Where/When' level.

Key Points

There are different types of group goals related to different levels of group process (who, why, how, what, where and when).

There are different types of strategies (operations and evidences) for addressing issues of 'want to', 'how to', 'chance to' and 'who to.'

Basic Attitudes and Filters of Experience: Meta Program Patterns

In many ways, meta program distinctions are more general versions of many of the processes we have already been exploring in this book. Meta program patterns are descriptions of the different ways in which a perceptual space, or elements of a perceptual space, may be approached. A list of them is provided in your manual.

As with the other distinctions we have explored, a person can apply the same meta program pattern regardless of content and context. Also, they are not "all or nothing" distinctions and may occur together in varying proportions.

Meta Program Patterns

In approaching a problem or idea, one can emphasize moving *"toward"* something or *"away from"* something, or some ratio of both. In a group, a problem or idea may be approached in varying degrees of proactivity and reactivity.

'*Chunk-size*' relates to the level of specificity or generality with which a person or group is analyzing a problem, idea or perceptual space. Concepts and situations may be analyzed in terms of varying degrees of detail (micro chunks of information) and generalities (macro chunks of information).

Problems and situations may be examined with reference to long term, medium term or short term time frames; and within the context of the past, present or future. The *time frame* within which a problem or idea is considered can greatly influence the way in which it is interpreted and approached. There might be both long term and short term implications.

Some people tend to look at history for solutions more so than the future. A good example is the difference between former Soviet leader Michail Gorbachev and the people who attempted to overthrow him before the break up of the Soviet Union. One was trying to prepare for the future, the others were trying to preserve the past.

Problems and situations may be considered in relation to the achievement of the *task*, or in relation to issues involving *relationship*, such as 'power' and 'affiliation'. The question of balance of focus with respect to task and relationship is obviously a key one with respect to managing a group. In the achievement of the task, either goals, procedures or choices may be emphasized. Issues involving relationship may be approached with an emphasis on the point of view of oneself, others or the context ('the company', 'the market', etc.) to varying degrees.

A problem or idea may be examined by comparing for similarities (*matching*) or differences (*mismatching*) of its elements. At the level of a group this relates to whether they are trying to reach consensus or encourage diversity.

Strategies for approaching problems and ideas may emphasize various combinations of vision, action, logic or emotion. Micro cognitive patterns on an individual level may be expressed in terms of a general *thinking style* on the macro level or group level. Vision, action, logic and emotion are more general expressions of visualization, movement, verbalization and feeling.

Different teaching and learning styles and approaches are characterized by different clusters and sequences of meta program patterns in various ratios. One person's approach might involve an 80% focus on relationship and 20% focus on task, and 70% emphasis on long-term versus 30% short-term considerations. Someone else may emphasize the task as 90% of the focus and think mostly in terms of short term considerations.

The different clusters of meta program patterns clearly cover different areas of perceptual space. In this respect, there are no 'right' or 'wrong' meta programs. Rather, their effectiveness in connection with learning and teaching relates to the ability to apply them to cover the space necessary to adequately deal with a problem or idea.

Different kinds of activities require different sorts of attitudes and approaches. Some activities require or emphasize the ability to focus on the micro chunks and details. Others require the ability to see the big picture. Different phases in the cycle of a group or team may call upon different thinking styles. Therefore, particular attitudes or clusters of meta program patterns might be more or less beneficial at different stages in a group's process. An emphasis on results more than procedures might either be a help or a constraint to a group's learning at different times. Some phases might require achieving consensus and at other phases it is important to encourage differences in perspectives.

Different thinking styles and approaches will have different values for different types of learning tasks. In conceptual learning, for example, it may be beneficial to direct thinking in terms of the big picture and a longer time frame. For developing procedural skill it may be more useful to be focused on short term actions. For analytical tasks it may be more appropriate to logically consider details with respect to the task, etc.

In this view, managing the process of a group essentially involves the pacing and leading of the different meta program patterns of the group members to fill in 'missing links' and widen the perception of the concept or idea.

Summary of Basic Attitudes and Filters of Experience Meta Program Patterns

Thinking Styles and Learning

1. **General approach**
   - Move 'away from' or 'towards' something
   - Be 'proactive' or 'reactive'

2. **Units of analysis**
   - Details - small information chunks
   - Generalities - large information chunks

3. **Time frame**
   - 'Short-term' or 'long-term'
   - Focus on past, present or future

4. **Basic cognitive style**
   - Vision
   - Action
   - Logic
   - Emotion

Key Points

Meta programs describe patterns in the ways people attend to and 'chunk' experiences, information or their perceptions of a situation.

Meta programs relate to different styles of sorting and filtering information and experiences.

Meta program patterns may be used to typify individuals, cultures or roles.

Identifying Basic Thinking Styles

The effective management of a group involves the continual recapitulation and incorporation of the different perspectives of all group members. Thus, when leading a group, it is important to maintain a balance between a) encouraging different perspectives and b) sharing an understanding of learning goals and issues.

There are two basic applications or motives for organizational learning: 1) to solve problems or 2) to establish or implement ideas. Implementing ideas and solving problems are interrelated processes that can be managed and balanced in a complementary manner. Generally, if the context is problem solving, the presenter's emphasis is on encouraging new perspectives. If the context is proposing and exploring a new idea, the emphasis is on synthesizing. That is, if the group is solving a problem, the presenter is seeking to promote different perspectives. If the group is implementing a new idea, the presenter is seeking commonalities and consensus.

Balance is a core criterion in managing the dynamics of a group. No one stage or thinking style should be favored at the expense of the others. Various thinking styles apply differently in achieving and implementing ideas versus solving problems. For example, Dreamer, Realist and Critic are not rigid personality types, but rather are tendencies within every person. There are general strategies and purposes for different thinking styles. For example:

The Dreamer is to widen perceptual space.

The Realist is to define actions.

The Critic is to evaluate payoffs and drawbacks.

There is a kind of dynamic balancing of processes that occurs in a group that can either be managed such that different thinking styles complement one another or it might be a conflict. And the question is, "Does it balance itself in a cycle that is productive or end up by polarizing the different thinking styles in a kind of 'Mexican standoff'?" These different functions and capabilities can either support each other or be destructive. A basic issue in managing a group is how you go about managing that dynamic balance within the group.

Thus, an important skill for a presenter is to be able to identify and respond appropriately to key patterns of thinking styles. One way to elicit key information about a person's thinking style is to ask questions relating to evaluations and decision making including relationships, successes, work and discretionary time. While meta program patterns are not related to specific words, linguistic patterns serve as important cues for meta program orientation. Styles may also be indicated through non-verbal signals such as vocal emphasis, gestures and body posture.

Exercise 10: Identifying Basic Thinking Styles

In this exercise, we will explore some issues relating to identifying and addressing different thinking styles.

Form a group of four. One person will be a presenter and the others will be group members.

1. Each group member chooses a different thinking styles to role play (e.g. dreamer, realist, critic). Group members are to choose a few patterns from the list of basic thinking styles in the previous unit. The group members should inform the presenter as to which thinking patterns they have chosen.

2. Presenter introduces a topic and manages a short discussion. The presenter should apply the various principles of communication and relationship explored up to this point. The objectives of the presenter should be to maintain a balanced interaction between the group members and keep them in a positive state.

3. After the discussion, the presenter guesses the thinking styles of different group members and the group is to discuss the impact of the different thinking styles on the discussion.

Skills Related to Managing a Group

Skills related to managing a group involve those related to managing task, relationship and context. Task-related skills tend to be finalized in results. Skill geared toward relationship and context are finalized in the effects on the group in terms of consensus, motivation and the group's state. Managing context involves dealing with several different elements including physical and non-physical parameters. In addition to 'physical environment', a 'context' is defined by the purpose of an interaction, assumption related to roles, policies and goals and constraints put on time or the use of physical space. Another important aspect of context is the stage of the learning cycle that the learners are in.

A key aspect in making a presentation and managing a group is the communication strategy adopted by the presenter. Our most fundamental definition of learning has been that it involves the establishment of cognitive maps, reference experiences and the connections between them. We have explored some of the processes and skills associated with effective teaching and learning, including:

1) the cognitive maps and perceptual channels used by the presenter

2) the physiology of the presenter and the group

3) the thinking and learning styles of group members and how they relate to different stages in the learning cycle

4) beliefs, values and role identity of the group members

All of these influences contribute to the effectiveness of groups as well as individuals. The communication strategy of a presenter involves the way in which he or she defines and directs these four key elements.

Representational channels are an important dimension of a presenter's communication strategy. Different representational channels and verbal patterns direct the cognitive processes of group members in different ways and influence the perceptions of a group's role relations. Different channels of communication and representation have different uses and strengths. An effective communication strategy matches the channels and modes of communication to accomplish different levels of goals and maintain rapport between group members.

We often make assumptions that others have the same cognitive capabilities that we do. But this is most often not the case. In communicating with others, matching their channel of representation is an important method of establishing rapport.

It is important to recognize that others have different thinking styles than our own. Sometimes a person is not used to visualizing even though people are talking about things that require the ability to remember or fantasize visually. At other times, a person might tend to focus too much on a particular image that has become imprinted in his or her mind. It stands out because it's unique or it's the only one that person has been exposed to. In challenging or stressful situations, people revert to their most familiar representational channel.

Thinking styles are expressed through different kinds of physiology. Recognizing the physiological cues associated with internal states and thinking styles is a very useful skill with which to direct or focus attention. At the level of a whole group, patterns of macro physiology, language and representational channels may be used to 'pace' and 'lead' the general thinking style of a whole group.

On a macro level, the 'state' of a person in a particular role is determined by that person's outcome plus his or her attitude. Attitude may be represented in terms of the cluster of meta program patterns the person manifests in relation to his or her goal. The success of a presenter relates to the presenter's abilities to match the needs and perceptions of the audience on a number of different levels including learning styles, values and role identity.

One of the principles of learning we have been exploring involves the importance of widening the coverage of a perceptual space. In that sense, no one meta program or meta program pattern or thinking style is right or wrong. The success of a group will be based on their ability to cover the appropriate issues within the perceptual space.

In forming a strategy for managing a group, it is important to realize that the role of an individual as a group member may be different from the role of that person in the larger organization. Sometimes when you are bringing together a new group, you might need to let roles develop. And, in a group, roles with respect to the learning process may not necessarily be related to function and role within the larger company or organization. There might be roles with respect to the organization and roles with respect to the group.

Basic Skills for Interacting With an Audience

There are a number of different interactive skills that are valuable for effectively managing a group's process:

° Keeping track of and monitoring the sequence of activities in the group.

° Acknowledging and directing different thinking styles (Such as Dreamer, Realist and Critic).

° Defining and monitoring the performance of individual and group T.O.T.E.s.

° Monitoring the overall T.O.T.E.s for task and relationship.

° Pacing and leading the a) physiology, b) thinking styles and c) values of group members.

° Identifying and filling in holes or missing links with respect to a) meta programs, b) levels of process and c) relevant perceptual positions.

° Using 'psychogeography' and behavioral cues to influence the interactive dynamics of the group.

° Sending and monitoring 'meta messages' to direct the level of communication, state and status.

° To provide and clarify information related to the context or frame of the group's task to provide focus for the group members.

Summary of Skills Related to Managing a Group

Skills Related to Managing a Group

Awareness of the learning cycle

Maintaining balance of task and relationship

Pacing and leading:
- Physiology
- Representational Channels
- Values

Responding to different:
- Thinking Styles
- Levels
- Points of view (perceptual positions)

Calibrating and monitoring non-verbal meta messages

Key Points

Skills related to managing a group involve those related to managing task, relationship and context.

Task-related skills are finalized in results.

Skills geared toward relationship and context are finalized in the effects on the group in terms of consensus, motivation and the group's state.

Exercise 11: 'Backtracking' and Active Listening

One way to apply the interactive skills of managing a group is through the process of 'active listening' and 'backtracking'.

Active listening involves paraphrasing and feeding back your understanding of what a person has said. For instance, if a group member asked, "What are some specific ways of pacing someone's thinking style?" the presenter would say something like, "I understand you would like some examples of how to match another person's thinking style." It is a useful way to acknowledge that you have heard the other person, plus it gives you a way to check your understanding of the map of the other person.

Backtracking is the process of reviewing, synopsizing, summarizing or sequentially recapitulating key points of an entire interaction. Rather than paraphrase the most recent communication of a single audience member, a presenter would backtrack by saying something like, "So, the key issues in our discussion have been a)...b)...c)..." In addition to the benefits of active listening, backtracking helps learners to continually keep track of the overall themes and frames and helps learners make and 'anchor' associations between key cognitive concepts.

Both active listening and backtracking give the presenter an opportunity to apply a number of the non-verbal and interactive skills we have explored in this book. While active listening or backtracking, the presenter may pace and lead certain audience members, establish anchors, emphasize certain points with non-verbal meta messages, calibrate the audience's reaction to certain topics and issues, etc.

The following exercise involves practicing the skills of active listening and backtracking.

1. Presenter introduces a topic to the group and takes questions.

2. The presenter is to 'backtrack' (active listening) the question before answering it and relate it to any relevant previous questions. The presenter may use this as an opportunity to practice some of the other non-verbal communication skill covered thus far in the book, such as:

- Acknowledging and directing different thinking styles.
- Pacing and leading the a) physiology, b) thinking styles and c) values of group members.
- Sending and monitoring 'meta messages' to direct the level of communication, state and status.
- Providing and clarifying information related to the context or frame of the group's task to provide focus for the group members.

3. At the end of the interaction, the presenter is to summarize all of the questions that were asked.

4. After the interaction, group members discuss the effects and benefits of the active listening and backtracking.

Summary of 'Backtracking' and Active Listening

Basic Skills for Interacting with an Audience

'Pacing and Leading'

Identifying and Matching Basic Thinking Styles

'Active Listening'
Paraphrasing Questions and
Comments 'Backtracking'

Key Points

There are a number of different ways in which a trainer may
facilitate and coordinate the learning process within a
group or team:
○ Acknowledging and directing the different styles of
thinking (Dreamer, Realist and Critic).
○ Pacing and leading the a) physiology, b) thinking styles
and c) values of group members.
○ Identifying and filling in holes or missing links with respect to a) meta programs, b) levels of process and c) relevant perceptual positions.
○ Using 'psychogeography' and behavioral cues to influence
the interactive dynamics of the group.

Process-Oriented Language Skills

One way to help 'match' a communication to someone's learning style is by using process words reflecting the particular sensory modality being experienced by the learner through his or her language patterns.

An individual's ongoing experience is comprised of some combination of each of his senses or "representational systems." Each person uses his auditory, visual, kinesthetic, and olfactory/gustatory senses to create his model of the world. Due to the influences in the personal backgrounds of individuals and the environments in which they develop their representational systems, there is a tendency for many people to develop or value the information processing capabilities of one of their representational systems to a greater degree than others. An auditorally-oriented person is one who prefers his or her ears in perception and who depends on spoken words for the information which is decisive in behavior. A visually-oriented person primarily uses his eyes to perceive the world around him, and uses visual images in remembering and in thinking. A kinesthetically-oriented person is one who feels her way through her experiences; both external and internal stimuli are sorted through her feelings and these feelings determine her decisions. Smell and taste are typically not primary senses, especially in presentation and organizational contexts, and so they will not be focused on in the following discussions and examples; however, this would include those who perceive the world through tastes or smells, such as cooks. The predominant representational system will often come out most obviously when a person is in a stressful state.

If a particular representational system is valued or developed more than the others, it can be either an asset or a limitation, depending on the flexibility one has in approaching or developing the others. Nevertheless, the representational system that is most highly valued will always greatly affect the way that a person perceives and acts upon the world.

Sensory-Based Predicates

A person's preferred sense can be identified by the predicates—adjectives, adverbs, verbs, and any other descriptive language—used in his or her speech. There is a revealing tendency for people to do what they are talking about. Through their language, people will literally tell you which representational systems they are employing to make sense of and organize their ongoing experience. In the following word groupings, examples of predicates are provided for each of the three basic senses:

Visual: I see what you are saying; that doesn't look quite right; I need to get clear on this idea; it's sort of hazy right now; I just go blank; that casts some light on the subject; we need a new perspective; a colorful example.

Auditory: That rings a bell; I hear you; it sounds good to me; listen to this; it just suddenly clicked; tune in to what they're trying to say; I had to ask myself; that idea has been rattling around in my head for a while.

Kinesthetic; I've got a good feeling about this project; get a handle on this; he needs to get in touch with the flow of the sentiment; a solid proposal; we're up against a wall; that's a heavy problem; can you grasp what needs to be done?

The table below lists some common language cues associated with the different representational modalities.

VISUAL	**AUDITORY**	**KINESTHETIC**
"see"	*"hear"*	*"grasp"*
"look"	*"listen"*	*"touch"*
"sight"	*"sound"*	*"feeling"*
"clear"	*"resonant"*	*"solid"*
"bright"	*"loud"*	*"heavy"*
"picture"	*"word"*	*"handle"*
"hazy"	*'noisy"*	*"rough"*
"brings to light"	*"rings a bell"*	*"connects"*
"show"	*"tell"*	*"move"*

Summary of Process Oriented Language Skills

Process-Oriented Language Skills

Matching Key Representational System Words

Representational Words Most Frequently Used

Visual	Auditory	Kinesthetic
'See'	'Hear'	'Grasp'
'Look'	'Listen'	'Touch'
'Sight'	'Sound'	'Feeling'
'Clear'	'Resonant'	'Solid'
'Bright'	'Loud'	'Heavy'
'Picture'	'Word'	'Handle'
'Hazy'	'Noisy'	'Rough'
'Brings to light'	'Rings a bell'	'Connects'
'Show'	'Tell'	'Move'

Key Points

One way to help 'match' a communication to someone's learning style is by using process words reflecting the particular sensory modality being experienced by the learner.

Certain language patterns indicate types and qualities of cognitive processes.

Clusters of physical clues give indications about which micro cognitive patterns are being mobilized and linked during a person's thinking process.

Pacing and Leading During a Group Discussion

One way of establishing rapport and acknowledging different thinking styles is by adapting one's own language to harmonize with people by appealing to their perceptual manner. This can be accomplished by two techniques—pacing and translating.

1. Pacing

As we have explored earlier in this book, pacing is the process of using and feeding back key behavioral cues to the other person. On a verbal level this involves echoing the most valued representational system of the other person by matching his or her predicates. It involves having the flexibility to pick up and incorporate the individual's vocabulary into one's own vocabulary.

For instance, one way to develop rapport is by listening to the kinds of language patterns a person uses and doing "active listening" by matching some of their words. So if somebody says, "I *feel* that we need to go more deeply into this," you might say, "Yes, I understand that you have a *feeling* that we need to explore this," instead of saying, "*Looks* to me like you want to *focus* on this more fully."

Sample conversations are probably the best way to clarify how this process works. The following transcripts of dialogue illustrate the function of pacing. The first transcript establishes how mis-communication occurs due to the lack of pacing between a "visual" presenter and a "kinesthetic" learner:

Visual: If you look over the presentation again I am sure you will see clearly that I've focused on all of the important issues. I don't see what's bothering you.

Kinesthetic: I just keep getting the feeling that something is missing. I can't put my finger on it, but there is something we need to get a better handle on.

Visual: I think you are stuck in your own point of view. If you looked at it from my perspective, you would be able to see how clear everything is.

Kinesthetic: I don't think you're getting in touch with the solid issues, and there could be some heavy problems if you don't come to grips with those.

It is apparent that these two people are talking right past each other—one using words that refer to what he sees, the other using words about how he feels. The next transcript exemplifies mis-communication between a "visual" learner and an "auditory" teacher.

Auditory: I want to talk with you because I've had some ideas rattling around in my head and I would like to find out how they sound to you.

Visual: Let me look at what you've got. Do you have them drawn up anywhere? What can you show me?

Auditory: Well, they are something I've just started to tune in to, and I wanted to use you as a sounding board. It's nothing to shout about, but I thought maybe we could play it by ear.

Visual: When you have something definite to show me then come back in. Once I can see that you have something worthwhile to look at, then we can focus on it.

Once again, mis-communication has occurred because neither person will recognize the representational system to which the other refers. This next transcript provides an example of pacing for each representational system:

Visual: As I look back over the presentation, I think there are some gray areas in it. I am not clear about what you were trying to say all along.

Pace: I think I can see what you are saying. Let me try to paint a picture of it so that I can illustrate my ideas a bit better. Then I am sure we will see eye-to-eye on it.

Auditory: I think we need to talk about this some more. I've listened to what you have had to say and it sounds like there might be some discord between what you're saying and what I'm thinking.

Pace: I think I can tune into what you're saying. I hear you. Let's replay our conversation for a minute and talk about what might be missing. Then maybe I can resonate with you on this.

Kinesthetic: I can't seem to get in touch with what you're saying. I feel as though I might just be spinning my wheels on this. I just can't get a handle on the meat of your presentation.

Pace: I think I can connect with you on that. I don't want to put you over a barrel on this, and my back is up against the wall, too. I'd like to take a little of the weight off, so let's walk back through the presentation and we'll try to find any soft spots.

Thus, by feeding back words that acknowledge and reflect the representational system used by the individual, communication and agreement can occur more rapidly and with greater ease.

2. Translating

"Translating" is the rephrasing of words from one representational system to another. It involves matching and mismatching predicates so that a "visual" begins to understand the world of a "kinesthetic," or an "auditory" that of a "visual." This technique especially applies to group discussions.

As before, a transcript of dialogue will be used to illustrate how the technique works. In this example, miscommunication has occurred between Barbara (a "visual") and Bill (a "kinesthetic"). The presenter is managing the discussion and translating the ideas using typical predicates to appeal to the different representational systems:

Barbara: He keeps showing me his idea but it looks so messy and scattered. I don't see how anything that looks this disorganized can improve our situation.

Bill: I think that she is insensitive to the things that are really important to people. This idea expresses the way a lot of people feel. If she wasn't so numb to people's feelings, she would be able to get in touch with how this can work.

Presenter: Barbara, I think that what Bill is trying to say is that you need to shift your perspective about this idea, and look past the details so that you can focus on the big picture. Then you'll see that there are certain issues that are going to stand out more clearly that others.
　　Bill, I think you've got to put yourself in Barbara's shoes. When she tries to connect with this the way it is presented, I think she feels that she is being pulled in all different directions, and there is nothing she feels she can hold on to. Keep the idea a bit more grounded and steady. Instead of rubbing her the wrong way, I think it would help things fall together more smoothly.

In this case the presenter acts literally as a translator, transferring the messages by using words that refer to the different representational systems.

Obviously these examples are highly exaggerated in terms of the amount of representational system language, but people do often express these different representational systems quite explicitly when asking questions and making comments.

Verbal Pacing of Representational Systems

The following exercise is a way to practice matching and mismatching a person's sensory language patterns.

1. B is to ask A to think of something A is very congruent about and something A is not totally congruent about, and to calibrate the differences in A's physiology.

2. B then asks A about something important to A. B keeps questioning A about the subject until A makes a response that indicates a particular representational system. (This is most easily done in the context of 'backtracking' or 'active listening'.)

3. Instead of 'backtracking', B is to paraphrase A's statement switching representational system predicates and check for congruence/incongruence.

e.g.
Statement: "I get satisfaction from my work when I *feel* I've helped someone get in *touch* with his or her own creativity."
Paraphrase #1: "So you get satisfaction from *seeing* yourself as a person who *shows* others their own creative abilities."
Paraphrase #2: "It's satisfying to you when people *tell* you you've been a *sounding board* for their own creativity?"

Exercise 12: Pacing And Leading During a Group Discussion

In the following exercise, readers will have the opportunity to explore the impact of process-oriented language. The presenter will practice pacing and/or leading the thinking style of others by utilizing their language patterns. The other group members will use language reflecting particular representational systems and will have the opportunity to experience how those words shape their perceptions.

Form small groups. One person will be the presenter and the others will be group members role playing people with different representational orientations.

1. Group members choose different representational modalities and language patterns to role play.

2. Presenter introduces a topic and manages a short discussion.

3. During the discussion the presenter is to attempt to:

   a) pace the language of each person
      and/or
   b) lead to a different or preferred representational channel chosen by the presenter

4. Group discusses the effect of the role play and the presenter's interventions. Group members should describe the effect of their language on their internal experience as well as the impact of the presenter's language.

Chapter 11

Managing Resistances or Interferences

Identifies and explores the communication and relational skills necessary to handle resistances and interferences within a group.

- **Motivation and Resistances with Respect to Learning**

- **Communication and Relational Skills for Managing Resistances and Interferences**

- **Some Principles for Dealing With Resistances and Interferences**

- **Making Observations in a Group**

- **Managing Different Thinking Styles in a Group**

Motivation and Resistance with Respect to Learning

Motivation and resistance are key issues in all aspects of the learning process. They influence learning in a number of important ways including the amount of effort learners invest in studying or attending, the amount of time they spend practicing the relevant skills and the degree of stress or anxiety they experience.

The Influence of Expectations on Motivation and Resistance

Motivation and resistance are shaped and influenced by one's values and expectations. There are several basic influences on a person's motivation to learn such as:

1. *Desirability of the Outcome.* The degree to which a learner values the consequences of, or results achieved through, the activity to be learned forms the basis of the external incentive for engaging the process of learning.
2. *Action-Outcome Expectation.* Motivation is influenced by the degree to which a person perceives that the skills he or she is performing actually produce benefits within the environmental system that constitutes his or her reality.
3. *Perceived Self-Efficacy.* The increase in one's perception of one's own personal effectiveness or adaptive capability is the internal motivation for learning and performing. On the other hand, a lack of perceived self efficacy can produce fear and resistance.

Since learning involves a person varying his or her behavior in order to achieve an outcome in the environment, beliefs and expectations about the desirability of an outcome, the actions it takes to achieve the desired outcome and one's own personal capabilities play an important role in the motivation to learn or change.

These kinds of beliefs and expectations influence how much effort people will expend, and how long they will sustain it in dealing with new or challenging situations. For instance, in self-managed activities, people who are skeptical of their ability to exercise adequate control over their actions tend to undermine their efforts in situations that tax capabilities.

In summary, the basic motivational space of learning involves beliefs and expectations relating to the fundamental components of change:

1. The desirability of the outcome.

2. Confidence that the specified actions will produce the outcome.

3. The evaluation of the appropriateness and difficulty of the behavior (regardless of whether it is believed it will produce the desired result).

4. The belief that one is capable of producing the required behaviors.

5. The sense of self worth or permission one has in relation to the required behaviors and outcome.

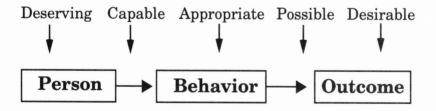

Areas of Beliefs Effecting Motivation to Learn

Motivational Issues with Respect to Presentations

To participate and perform maximally, a learner must a) **want to** be involved in the learning process, b) know **how to** activate and apply the relevant skills and strategies with respect to the learning instruments and procedures, and c) get the **chance to** demonstrate and apply the required skills. A person is not likely to perform well if he does not want to and cannot do so if he does not know what to do or is not given the opportunity.

'*Wanting to*' relates to beliefs, values and expectations. If a learner does not understand the purpose of a learning goal or activity, he or she will likely resist because it will not be perceived as either appropriate or desirable. If a learner does not believe it is possible to meet the standards set for performance, he or she will likely be apathetic. If a learner does not believe he or she has the capability to perform well, he or she will likely experience stress and anxiety.

'*Knowing how to*' relates the learner's conscious and un-conscious competence with the skills to be learned and the learner's clarity and familiarity with the learning instruments and procedures. In addition to the amount and quality of training material, cognitive maps and reference experiences that have been provided for the learner, the learner's performance is influenced by his or her previous experience and familiarity with the learning procedures.

Getting the '*chance to*' relates to the learning context and environment. The degree of relational support one receives, the amount of variability in the system and the tools one has available, will determine the probability that a capability will be able to be internalized and applied. Constraints, interferences or lack of support can prevent a learner from performing optimally in a particular learning environment.

Dealing with motivation and resistance during a presentation essentially involves dealing with these issues of wanting to, knowing how to and providing the chance to.

Summary of Motivation and Resistance with Respect to Learning

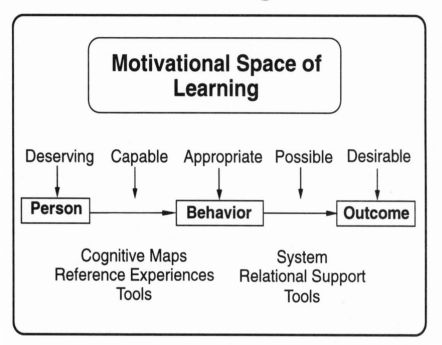

Key Points

The basic motivational space of learning involves beliefs and expectations relating to the fundamental components of change:

1. The desirability of the outcome.
2. Confidence that the specified actions will produce the outcome.
3. The evaluation of the appropriateness and difficulty of the behavior.
4. The belief that one is capable of producing the required behaviors.
5. The sense of self worth or permission one has in relation to the required behaviors and outcome.

Communication and Relational Skills for Managing Resistances and Interferences

The dynamics of a group are shaped by context, attitude, states, cognitive processes, communication channels and rules of interaction between group members. A presenter can establish an environment or context that helps widen or restrict the participation of the audience.

It is possible to structure a framework which would encourage, or maybe unintentionally inhibit, different kinds of thinking styles. For example, setting a particular time frame might in and of itself bring out or inhibit a Dreamer, Realist, or Critic response. For instance, if a presenter said "I want to know your best dream: you each have one minute!" this might be contradictory to the process he or she is actually trying to encourage. When you say, "OK everybody we have 5 more minutes," it is more likely to draw out the Realist than the Dreamer.

As an analogy, Walt Disney had a special room set up just to encourage the 'dreamer' style of thinking. In the dreaming room, there weren't any tables. And inspirational pictures were plastered all over the walls of the room. He did not allow any criticisms or negative thinking to be expressed in the room.

There are different kinds of operations that help to inter-actively stimulate and manage the participation of a group:

° Having people participate by stimulating more physical actions.

° Underlining what is common and what is different between different perspectives.

° Asking questions, expressing doubts and approval, and provoking new perspectives.

° Giving tools, instruments and resources.

° Giving feedback, making proposals, asking for the integration and synthesis of ideas.

° Switching communication channels by writing, using flip charts, blackboards, etc.

Thus, there are certain constraints and rules of interaction that might favor the widest associations and expression of ideas and perspectives; for instance, not having a defined time frame for a discussion and not disqualifying even seemingly 'stupid' questions. A presenter can also take off the constraints of reality by encouraging exaggeration and "as if" thinking by saying, "Even if you can't imagine it, act as if you can." It is also helpful to encourage the use of metaphors and symbolic language as we have explored in earlier chapters.

If problems arise or there is resistance in the group, there are a number of ways in which a presenter can influence the group members to reengage their participation.

° Reframing the problem or goal from a different point of view.

° Reprioritizing criteria or values.

° Changing level of focus and finding limiting assumptions.

° Looking for 'missing links'.

° Chunking down to set sub goals, or dealing with partial areas of perceptual space.

° Changing perspectives or states (by using humor, for example).

° Switching representational channels and encouraging lateral thinking.

° Encouraging "as if" thinking.

Meta Communication

Another useful strategy to manage resistances or interferences is the process of Metacommunication. Metacommunication is 'communication about communication'. Metacommunication is a more macro level process than sending a metamessage. A meta communication is often a verbal statement that sets a framework around a communication situation in the form of rules, guidelines and expectations. It essentially involves setting the frame for an interaction. The presenter metacommunicates about the situation to set up appropriate expectations and presuppositions in the group. Before a presenter begins a presentation or discussion, he or she may decide to set certain guidelines, rules of interaction, rules of interpretation, etc.

Metamessages are a sort of subtext that emphasize certain aspects of a message non-verbally. For example, if a person says "YOU weren't respecting the rules," emphasizing the "You" with voice inflection, it marks the communication as an identity level message. Saying, "You weren't respecting the RULES," emphasizes the level of why and how.

Metacommunication, on the other hand, would be saying something like, "Why do we have this rule?" "What's the goal and purpose of the rule?" And initiating a discussion *about* the rules. Metacommunication might be saying something like, "It's important for us to do this," or "The rule helps you to do that." The group might actually have a discussion about the rule instead of emphasizing the various levels of experience involved in breaking the rule. So the metacommunication clarifies the framework of the communication.

When a presenter is going into a very different culture, he or she might spend quite a bit of time metacommunicating before actually beginning a presentation or discussion to set the frameworks for people to accurately interpret both verbal and non-verbal messages. If one doesn't provide any reference points, one can only hope that people share a similar enough culture to interpret messages appropriately.

A study was made of the communication patterns of effective leaders and it was observed that almost half of the leaders' communication was metacommunication. Effective leaders were constantly saying things like, "I'm going to be talking about this..." "This is how I want you to think about it." "Focus here..." "Have these types of expectations." It is as if they were setting up a whole structure before they finally made the one essential point. Because the interpretation and understanding of that one point was so significant, they needed to cover all the perceptual space around it so there was no ambiguity.

The amount of metacommunication is a strategic choice. For example, when a presenter goes into a new situation, he or she might spend more time metacommunicating than when the presenter is going into a familiar situation.

Meta communication also involves 'talking about' what is happening during a communication interaction in order to make conscious or acknowledge some significant event. Therefore, if a presenter feels that there is something going on in a group that seems ambiguous or that there is an undercurrent or something else going on, then he or she might choose to go back and clarify some of the issues or assumptions by metacommunication about the situation.

Summary of Communication and Relational Skills for Managing Resistances and Interferences

Communication and Relational Skills for Managing Resistances and Interferences

- **Taking 'Second Position'**

- **Responding to 'Positive Intentions'**

- **'Reframing'**

Key Points

When problems or interferences arise during the group learning process, there are a number of strategies the trainer can use to help widen or open up perceptual space.

° Reframing the problem or goal from a different point of view
° Reprioritizing criteria or values
° Changing level of focus and finding limiting assumptions
° Looking for 'missing links'
° Chunking down to set sub goals, or dealing with parts of an idea or learning task
° Changing perspectives or states (by using humor, for example)
° Switching representational channels and encouraging lateral thinking
° Encouraging "as if" thinking

Some Principles for Dealing with Resistances and Interferences

There are some important principles to keep in mind that are valuable to help deal with resistances and problems during a presentation.

1. *The map is not the territory.* As human beings, we can never know reality. We can only know our perceptions of reality. We experience and respond to the world around us primarily through our sensory representational systems. It is our maps of reality that determine how we behave and that give those behaviors meaning, not reality itself. It is generally not reality that limits us or empowers us, but rather our map of reality.

2. *Life and 'mind' are systemic processes.* The processes that take place within a human being and between human beings and their environment are systemic. Our bodies, our societies, and our universe form an ecology of complex systems and sub-systems, all of which interact with and mutually influence each other. It is not possible to completely isolate any part of the system from the rest of the system. Such systems are based on certain 'self-organizing' principles and naturally seek optimal states of balance or homeostasis.

3. *At some level, all behavior is adaptive or "positively intended."* That is, it is or was perceived as appropriate given the context in which it was established, from the point of view of the person whose behavior it is. People make the best choices available to them given the possibilities and capabilities that they perceive to be accessible within their model of the world. Any behavior, no matter how evil, crazy or bizarre it seems, is the best choice available to that person at that point in time.

Wisdom, ethics and ecology do not derive from having the one 'right' or 'correct' map of the world, because human beings are not capable of making one. Rather, the goal is to create the richest map possible that respects the systemic nature and ecology of ourselves and the world in which we live.

Thus, in dealing with resistances and problems in a group, it is important and useful to:

1) Presuppose that all behavior is positively intended.

2) Separate the negative aspects of the behavior from the positive intent behind it.

3) Identify and respond to the positive intent of the resistant/problem person.

4) Offer the person other choices of behavior to achieve the same positive intent.

Summary of Some Principles for Dealing with Resistances and Interferences

Some Principles for Dealing with Resistances and Interferences

- The map is not the territory. Everyone has a different world view and there is no one 'right' model of the world.

- Knowing other people's maps is useful in order to communicate and interact with them effectively.

- People make the best choices available to them given the possibilities and capabilities they perceive accessible to them.

- It is important to separate a person's behavior from the positive intention behind it, and respond to the intention.

- Resistances and objections are often communications about positive intentions that are not being satisfied.

Key Points

In dealing with resistances and problems in a group, it is important and useful to presuppose that:

1) All behavior is positively intended.

Key Points (continued)

2) The negative aspects of the behavior are separate from the positive intent behind it.

3) It is best to identify and respond to the positive intent of the resistant/problem person.

4) One can offer the person other choices of behavior to achieve the same positive intent.

Making Observations in a Group

Observing dynamic patterns within groups involves a different focus than observing individuals. It is a crucial skill for presenters. Observing patterns of the language and behavior of others is an important way to solidify what you have learned and assess what you know.

The final exercise described in the following chapter provides an opportunity to observe the dynamic patterns in a group. It is structured such that several groups of observers watch a role play in what is known as a 'Fish bowl'. One group of observers will focus on patterns of physiology. There are two aspects of physiology to pay attention to: the micro aspects and the macro aspects. On a micro level, observers might notice a meta message someone is giving in a particular moment about what that person is sending or receiving. Leaning toward, leaning away, gesturing, etc., are different types of behavioral cues that are meta messages. These will occur in some particular moment as some kind of feedback about the individual experience or response to what is happening. It can be very important to be able to track how someone's physiology changes in response to a particular stimulus. These observers will want to look for not only the kinds of clues individual role players express but also how those clues change based upon interventions by the team leader. They should notice how the presenter either consciously or unconsciously uses physiology, such as posture or gestures, to trigger or shape the direction of the group process.

In addition to key behavioral cues given by individual members of the group, it is important to observe how cues change relative to the presenter's interventions and to the responses of other group members. It is also important to observe how the presenter utilizes these cues to 'calibrate' and lead the group. Observers should pay attention to how the presenter himself uses his or her physiology to either show neutrality to certain communications, or possibly to form an alliance with different people at different times through the process of mirroring or pacing and leading. Empathy toward a particular person or perspective might be shown through the body, which then becomes a message to others in the group.

On a macro level, observers might notice patterns of physiology and movement between people. For example, the amount of activity as it travels back and forth between group members might be an indication of how much people are participating. Macro level behavioral patterns are an evidence about the group as opposed to a meta message about a particular individual.

A second group of observers is to pay attention to the cognitive patterns and the thinking styles expressed by the individuals. Which representational channels are being used by the different individuals? What kinds of things are being represented verbally, logically? In addition to the kind of language that a person is using, somebody might draw something, using a visual channel, or switch to a more metaphorical mode of representation.

A third group of observers is to pay attention to meta program patterns. How do group members punctuate events in terms of their approach towards, away, generalities, details, past/future, long-term/short-term, etc.? In addition to noticing which meta program patterns are emphasized by different individuals, it is relevant to observe in what sequence they unfold and in what ways individuals shift or exaggerate meta programs in relation to the meta programs of others.

The fourth group of observers is to pay attention to how levels of process are expressed or addressed in terms of *where, when, what, how, why, who.* In particular, they should watch and listen for how different role-players give inputs or responses on different levels. For instance, one individual might focus his or her words at the level of the *what.* Another might focus at the level of how or why. In addition to observing which specific individuals give cues about the different levels (what, how, why, who, etc.), it is useful to observe in what sequence issues relating to different levels are raised and addressed and in what order the presenter manages issues related to levels.

Notice how the presenter either consciously or unconsciously addresses or responds to the different levels of focus. In terms of managing the group, for example, does the presenter focus first on why, who, what, etc.? In observing the dynamics of a group, it is especially relevant to notice how different levels of process are managed. A key skill of a presenter is to determine which levels are relevant to manage given a particular perceptual space and group of individuals. The thoroughness with which the different levels are covered often determines the degree of alignment of group members with respect to both task and relationship. Thoroughness of coverage is based on a) which levels are covered, b) how deeply each level is covered (i.e., self - others, long term - short term, what is being approached - what is being avoided, etc.), and c) how many group members are involved in defining each level.

The purpose of making observations in a group is not to judge the performance of the presenter or group members but rather to contribute to the awareness of the group process for all group members (including other observers).

Individuals involved in a group process may also move into an observer position during or after a group process in order to develop meta cognition and expand their map of the situation.

Summary of Making Observations in a Group

Observing Dynamic Patterns of a Group

Physiology:
- What cues are given by each member?
- How do they change relative to the presenter's interventions?
- How does the presenter use these and other cues to stimulate/lead the group?

Representational channels:
- Which group members use which primary representational channels?
- How does the presenter 'manage' the use of representational channels (pacing versus leading)?

Logic levels:
- Who focuses on the what, how, why?
- How does the presenter 'manage' the levels (which ones first, which ones later)?

Thinking styles:
- What thinking styles are 'used' by each member?
- What interaction patterns are there between members?
- How do thinking styles of one member shift in response to the messages and meta messages of another member?

Key Points

Observing patterns of the language and behavior of others is an important way to learn and assess what you know. It is also a crucial skill for trainers.

Observing dynamic patterns within groups involves a different focus than observing individuals.

In addition to key micro and macro behavioral cues given by individual members of the group, it is important to observe how they change relative to the trainer's interventions and to the responses of other group members. It is also important to observe how the trainer utilizes these cues to 'calibrate' and lead the group.

In addition to observing which specific individuals give cues about the different levels (what, how, why, who, etc.), it is useful to observe in what sequence issues relating to different levels are raised and addressed and in what order the trainer manages issues related to levels.

In addition to noticing which meta program patterns are emphasized by different individuals, it is relevant to observe in what sequence they unfold and in what ways individuals shift or exaggerate meta programs in relation to the meta programs of others.

Managing Different Thinking Styles in a Group

An important communication and relational skill is to be able to identify and match or influence the thinking style of audience members. A key consideration for a presenter is how to anticipate and 'package' information to fit different thinking styles. Managing different thinking styles is especially pertinent during interactive discussions.

Knowing the thinking style of the audience ahead of time can make a difference in the strategy of the presenter. If the thinking styles are not known, the presenter must attend more to the audience. If the thinking styles are known, the presenter can do more preplanning and focus more on the strategy.

It is important for the presenter to develop the capability to take 'second position' with a number of different thinking styles (such as Dreamer, Realist and Critic) in order to be able to understand and direct the learning process of group members. The fundamental principles for effectively directing the activity of a group toward a common goal are 'pacing and leading' and 'acknowledging and adding'.

'Dreamer', 'Realist' and 'Critic' provides a typology of common thinking styles relevant to the presentation environment. Presenters are often more at ease with one style than the others. Particular thinking styles are not so much a personality type as they are an expression of the tendency of an individual to enact or express a certain attitude or meta program in a group. This tendency is often shaped by dynamic influences coming from other group members and the presenter.

In the next exercise we are going to explore the application of the skills you have been developing to a situation involving individuals with different thinking styles. The focus of the activity is to explore how to apply some of the models and distinctions to managing the group's learning process. The presenter is going to present a challenging learning task and handle any resistances that arise. The objective for the presenter is to acknowledge and draw out each thinking style in such a way that it contributes constructively to the group's learning process.

Another useful skill for a presenter, especially in relation to dealing difficult or challenging situations, is the skill of 'meta position'. 'Meta position' is an observer position in which one observes oneself as well as others. Meta position is a useful process to facilitate awareness and 'meta communication'. In a 'meta position' one leaves one's role in an interaction and becomes an observer to oneself. Reviewing one's behavior from an observer perspective leads to a different perspective and new awareness.

The purpose of the role play is to explore in more detail the kinds of issues and operations that might be involved in coordinating different thinking styles around the achievement of a challenging learning task. The exercise involves four role-players who will enact a situation in front of the rest of the group in a "fish bowl" format. The rest of the group will be assigned different kinds of patterns to watch and listen for. One group will look at physiology; another will be looking for the different levels of interaction; another will observe for kinds of meta programs and thinking styles.

This format is often very effective for integrating the learnings that have been accumulating throughout the course and deepening insight into the kinds of micro skills that are useful for managing the process of a group. Interactive practice often brings out both unconscious competence and unconscious incompetence. Role plays provide a way in which many of the skills, distinctions and principles of managing group process can be experientially demonstrated, evaluated and refined. Role playing is another form of acting "as if" which engages a high commitment of 'neurology' without having to get too involved in the content. Role plays often have a symbolic value that enhances other levels of learning.

In enacting the role play, it is a good idea make the task something that is familiar enough so that the role players do not need any special technical knowledge.

The roles include a presenter and individuals with thinking styles of Dreamer, Realist and Critic. Role playing different thinking styles can provide further insight into the experience of others.

The role players will have 5 minutes to prepare, using the cluster of meta program listed below as a guide to enacting the appropriate attitude and thinking style.

	Dreamer	Realist	Critic
	What	*How*	*Why*
Representational Preference	Vision	Action	Logic
Approach	Toward	Toward	Away
Time Frame	Long Term	Short Term	Long/Short Term
Time Orientation	Future	Present	Past/Future
Reference	Internal - Self	External - Environment	External - Others
Mode of Comparison	Match	Match	Mismatch

The objective of the presenter for this 15 minutes is to try to coordinate the different thinking styles and stimulate all of the group to understand and participate in the task.

The role-play itself will proceed in 10-15 chunks with pauses for observations from the observers. The 10-15 minute time frame is to allow for a long enough interaction to get some examples of patterns on a micro-interactive level, but not to go so long that the observers become overwhelmed.

Summary of Managing Different Thinking Styles in a Group

'Fish Bowl' Exercise: Presentation role play

Goal: to present a challenging learning task and address any resistance

Roles:
- Presenter: Manages group dynamics
- Dreamer
- Critic
- Realist

Four groups of observers keep track of different cues.
1. Physiology
2. Representational channels
3. Logical levels
4. Thinking styles

Key Points

A key consideration for a presenter is how to anticipate and 'package' information to fit different thinking styles.

If a presenter knows he or she is appealing to a particular thinking style, he or she should anticipate and prepare for the reactions of the others.

Key Points (continued)

Pacing and leading is the most effective way to manage different thinking styles.

Interactive practice often brings out both unconscious competence and unconscious incompetence.

Role playing different thinking styles can provide further insight into the experience of others.

Chapter 12

Conclusion

Principles of Effective Presentations

The objective for this book has been to explore some of the principles and patterns related to making effective presentations in a learning context. Learning involves the creation of cognitive maps formed from our inner representations and from language and then connecting them to reference experiences. By identifying key patterns relating to internal representations, language and physiology, we have developed a set of tools with which to enhance communication skills related to effective presentations.

As situations change, we need to adjust how we deal with them in order to respond effectively. Processes that produce a result in one situation may not produce the same result in a different context. Elements of the process need to be added or adapted. So, a certain minimum amount of flexibility is needed to manage change within the systems of which we are a member.

We began by exploring some of the basic skills of presenting and exploring some of your own conscious and unconscious competence associated with making presentations. We concluded that effective performances involved setting goals. If there's no direction or outcome for one's actions, it's difficult to be effective. In other words, if you only know what you don't want, and you don't know what you do want, it is difficult to act effectively.

We further concluded that effective performance also involves establishing evidences for the achievement of goals. An effective presentation takes place through a feedback loop between goals, ideas, actions and perceptions. The T.O.T.E. model is a way to organize one's presentations in terms of the goals, evidence procedures, operations and response to problems that characterize an effective process.

We then explored how to utilize some of the various types of representational channels and reference experience. We established that the different channels by which we make and communicate cognitive maps can either open up perceptual spaces or create confusion, and explored the value of alternative modes of representation such as metaphor and symbolic expressions.

We established the importance of connecting cognitive maps to meaningful reference experiences and the relevance of the skill of 'anchoring' to that process. We also established the importance of the internal state of the audience and the relevance of observational skills of the presenter in relation to 'calibrating' both macro and micro behavior of cues of an audience.

The presenter's relationship and rapport with an audience is another significant factor that can be facilitated by the skills of 'pacing and leading' and taking 'second position'. Both communication and relationship may be greatly enhanced by the presenter's ability to manage both verbal and non-verbal communication and relate messages with their accompanying meta messages.

In addition to their attention on their audience, effective presenters must also apply certain 'self-skills' relating to the management of their own internal state and their ability to effectively plan and prepare their presentations. The techniques of 'contrastive analysis' and the 'circle of excellence' are powerful tools for a presenter to manage his or her own state. Disney's creative cycle of dreamer, realist and critic can not only help presenters to effectively plan presentations, but also provides a useful way to categorize different thinking and learning styles.

We have acknowledged the fact that different people have different styles and strategies for learning and presenting. One essential skill in making effective presentations involves interacting with people who have different types of learning strategies. Another key skill involves coordinating different kinds of teaching and learning styles. Some styles and strategies are effective for certain situations and not for others. One goal of this book is to suggest ways in which we can enhance and increase the communication and relational skills within ourselves and others. By interacting with other people who have different strategies, you can find elements that enrich your own abilities.

The processes of 'backtracking' and 'matching and translating' key words used by members of an audience are basic skills for managing a group.

Managing resistance and motivation in an audience is based upon the presenter's ability to identify key areas of beliefs in group members and separate their behavior from their positive intentions.

Some Operational Principles of Effective Communication

As a summary, we can define three general operational principles of effective presentations:

1. Outcome Frame—Maintain an orientation toward the future goal that you want to achieve rather than away from the problem to be avoided. Even if you are trying to get around a problem, it is important to do it within the broader vision and context of the goal state.

2. Feedback versus Failure Frame—If a particular approach doesn't work, the way in which it failed will give you feedback as to what to do to succeed (learn from your mistakes). Sometimes you even need to do something which you know will not work in order to get the feedback necessary to take the next step.

3. Flexibility Frame-a)—Always have at least two other choices to fall back on before you start implementing a particular operation; b) "If what you are doing isn't working, do something different-do anything different." Almost anything is a better choice than what you are doing if you've already demonstrated that it won't work.

The first general principle is that effective presentations are goal-oriented. Even if the purpose of the presentation relates to avoiding something, you need to avoid it with reference to some kind of goal. In other words, even if you try to get around a problem, it needs to be done in a wider context of a desired state.

The second general principle is that an effective presentation requires a feedback versus a failure frame. Learning is an ongoing process that requires feedback. Depending upon the nature of the outcome, it may take more or less to accomplish a particular goal. It is important to distinguish between the process and the results of learning. Learning isn't just related to immediate results, it is a function of an ongoing feedback loop. Sometimes you even need to do something that you know probably won't work in order to get the feedback necessary to progress.

The third general principle is that of flexibility. It's often useful to have choices already planned before you start something, so you're not having to reflexively respond to problems. Effective presentations involve having a range of possibilities before you begin. The flexibility principle is also related to the 'law of requisite variety' in systems theory. It is important to have a degree of variability proportional to the possible change or uncertainty in the system. Stated simply, "If what you're doing isn't working, do something different." Do anything different, because if you have already demonstrated that what you're doing is not working, there is no purpose to continue proving it to yourself. Almost anything is a better choice than what you're doing.

Implications of the Flexibility Principle

An important implication with regard to flexibility in communication is that THERE IS NO SUCH THING AS RESISTANT STUDENTS OR LEARNERS, THERE ARE ONLY INFLEXIBLE PRESENTERS, INSTRUCTORS, TRAINERS, ETC. Have you ever tried to talk to someone but found you were not getting through to him or her? If you find a barrier such as this, try another approach. As soon as there is a behavior you can't perform, there is a response you can't elicit. IF WHAT YOU ARE DOING IS NOT GETTING THE OUTCOME YOU WANT, THEN DO SOMETHING DIFFERENT. And although these principles may sound like simple common sense, you would be surprised at how many people get stuck doing one or two techniques over and over again because they worked once before.

A final principle to keep in mind when you are establishing outcomes and varying your behavior is that THE MEANING OF YOUR COMMUNICATION IS THE RESPONSE YOU ELICIT, REGARDLESS OF WHAT YOU INTENDED BY THAT COMMUNICATION. Sometimes when a person is trying to be helpful or thoughtful, for instance, the other person may misinterpret it or respond adversely to it. Rather than be angry or hurt in such a situation, DO SOMETHING DIFFERENT. The people we communicate with cannot read our minds. If a person responds with irritation or mistrust, then that is the meaning of the communication to that person, and if you want a different response, vary your behavior until you elicit a different response that fits your desired outcome.

The great Greek philosopher Aristotle maintained that an effective speaker had to have three basic abilities "(1) to reason logically, (2) to understand human character, and (3) to understand emotions." These capabilities appear to be just as relevant today as they were twenty five hundred years ago. The purpose of this book has been to help you develop some of the key skills which support these abilities. I hope they will serve you well.

Summary of Principles of Effective Presentations

Summary of Some General Principles of Presentation

- **People learn by connecting cognitive maps to reference experiences.**

- **Cognitive maps are made of sensory and language representations.**

- **Reference experiences are made of remembered, ongoing or constructed experiences.**

- **Any effective learning process or presentation has a structure consisting of:**

  - a goal
  - evidences (assessments as to the outcomes),
  - operations to move toward the goal.

Key Points

Learning relates to how we construct our maps of the world.

Because situations change, we must continually adjust our maps.

Maps that are effective in one context may be ineffective in another.

Our maps have a structure based on cognitive, linguistic and physiological patterns.

Our thinking processes are oriented around a basic goal oriented feedback loop called a T.O.T.E.

Summary of Principles of
Effective Presentations (continued)

Some Basic Operational Principles of Effective Presentations

1. **The outcome principle:**
   - Goals stimulate and direct activity.

2. **The feedback principle:**
   - There is no failure, only feedback.

3. **The flexibility principle, the Law of Requisite Variety:**
   - If what you are doing isn't working, do something different.

Key Points

On a macro level there are some basic principles and attitudes related to the an effective teaching/learning process.

While the stimulus for learning something may either be to achieve or to avoid, its effectiveness is result of reaching a positive outcome or a solution space.

Key Points (continued)

Within the frame of learning there are no failures. Rather, lack of success is perceived as either a) a solution to different problem, or b) feedback providing information about what needs to be adjusted or how it needs to be adjusted.

Learning is deeply related to finding new choices. Having several options before starting something is important. Having a choice is always better than not having one.

If what you are doing is not working, then do something different.

Bibliography

Skills for the Future, Dilts, R. & Bonissone, G.; Meta
Publications, Capitola, California, 1993.

*Tools for Dreamers: Strategies for Creativity and the
Structure of Invention*, Dilts, R. B., Epstein, T., Dilts,
R. W., Meta Publications, Cupertino, Ca.,1991.

Applications of NLP, Dilts, R.; Meta Publications,
Capitola, California, 1983.

*Neuro-Linguistic Programming: The Study of the
Structure of Subjective   Experience, Volume I* ;
Dilts, R., Grinder, J., Bandler, R., DeLozier, J.; Meta
Publications, Capitola, California, 1980.

Walt Disney; The Dreamer, The Realist and The Critic,
Dilts, R., Dynamic Learning Publications, Ben Lomond,
Ca.,1990.

"Overcoming Resistance to Persuasion with NLP", Dilts, R.,
Joseph Yeager, 1990, Dynamic Learning Publications,
Ben Lomond, Ca.

*"The Parable of the Porpoise: A New Paradigm for Learning
and Management"*, Dilts, R., Dynamic Learning
Publications, Ben Lomond, Ca., 1990.

"Let NLP Work for You ", Dilts, R., 1982, **Real Estate
Today** , February, 1982, Volume 15, November 2.

*"Neuro-Linguistic Programming in Organizational
Development "*, Dilts, R., 1979, Organizational
Development Network Conference Presentation Papers,

New York, New York.

"NLP In Training Groups", Dilts, R., Epstein, T., Dynamic Learning Publications, Ben Lomond, Ca., 1989.

Plans and the Structure of Behavior, Miller, G., Galanter, E., and Pribram, K., Henry Holt & Co., Inc., 1960.

Principles of Psychology, William James, *Britannica Great Books,* Encyclopedia Britannica Inc., Chicago Ill., 1979.

On the Soul, Aristotle, *Britannica Great Books,* Encyclopedia Britannica Inc., Chicago Ill., 1979.

Mind and Nature, Bateson, Gregory; E. P. Dutton, New York, NY, 1979.

Steps To an Ecology of Mind, Bateson, G.; Ballantine Books, New York, New York, 1972.

Cybernetics, Wiener, N., The M.I.T. Press, Cambridge, MASS, 1965.

Introduction to Cybernetics, Ashby, W. Ross, Chapman & Hall, Ltd., London, England, 1956.

Design for a Brain, Ashby, W. Ross, Chapman & Hall, Ltd., London, England, 1960.

Models of Teaching; Bruce Joyce and Marsha Weil, Prentice Hall, Inc., Englewood Cliffs, New Jersey, 1986.

Teaching Thinking Skills; Baron, J., Sternberg, R. (Editors), W. H. Freeman and Comapny, New York, NY, 1987.